MARQUEE SERIES

Microsoft® Office

2016
Brief Edition

Workbook

Nita Rutkosky
Pierce College Puyallup
Puyallup, Washington

Audrey Roggenkamp
Pierce College Puyallup
Puyallup, Washington

Ian Rutkosky
Pierce College Puyallup
Puyallup, Washington

PARADIGM
EDUCATION SOLUTIONS

St. Paul

Senior Vice President	Linda Hein
Editor in Chief	Christine Hurney
Director of Production	Timothy W. Larson
Production Editors	Rachel Kats, Jen Weaverling
Cover and Text Designer	Valerie King
Copy Editor	Sarah Kearin
Senior Design and Production Specialist	Jaana Bykonich
Assistant Developmental Editors	Mamie Clark, Katie Werdick
Testers	Desiree Carvel; Ann E. Mills, Ivy Tech Community College of Indiana, Indianapolis, IN
Instructional Support Writer	Brienna McWade
Indexer	Terry Casey
Vice President Information Technology	Chuck Bratton
Digital Projects Manager	Tom Modl
Vice President Sales and Marketing	Scott Burns
Director of Marketing	Lara Weber McLellan

Care has been taken to verify the accuracy of information presented in this book. However, the authors, editors, and publisher cannot accept responsibility for Web, email, newsgroup, or chat room subject matter or content, or for consequences from application of the information in this book, and make no warranty, expressed or implied, with respect to its content.

Trademarks: Microsoft is a trademark or registered trademark of Microsoft Corporation in the United States and/or other countries. Some of the product names and company names included in this book have been used for identification purposes only and may be trademarks or registered trade names of their respective manufacturers and sellers. The authors, editors, and publisher disclaim any affiliation, association, or connection with, or sponsorship or endorsement by, such owners.

Cover Photo Credits: © whitehoune/Shutterstock.com; © Photobank gallery/Shutterstock.com.

Information Technology Essentials Photo Credits: Page ITE-1: Image 1, © Photobank/Shutterstock.com and Image 2, © iStockphoto.com/Whitehoune, page 8 (header); Page ITE-2: (top) © iStockphoto.com/Andrew Parfenov, (middle) © iStockphoto.com/Neustockimages, (bottom) courtesy of Epson America, Inc.; Page ITE-3: (top) © iStockphoto.com/darren wise, (bottom left) © iStockphoto.com/Oleksiy Mark, (bottom right) courtesy of Motorola; Page ITE-4: (top) courtesy of McKesson Provider Technologies, (middle) courtesy of SanDisk Corporation, (bottom) courtesy of Intel Corporation; Page ITE-5: (top) courtesy of ASUSTeK Computer Inc., (bottom) © Alexey Rotanov / Shutterstock; Page ITE-6: (top) courtesy of Logitech, (middle) courtesy of Western Digital Corp., (bottom) courtesy of Verbatim Americas LLC.; Page ITE-8: (top) used with permission from Microsoft Corporation; Page ITE-11: (bottom left) © iStockphoto.com/killerb10, (bottom right) courtesy of Intuit Inc.; Page ITE-12: (top) courtesy of Opera Software APA; Page ITE-16 (middle) © iStockphoto.com/ nolimitpictures, (bottom) © iStockphoto.com/Sebastien Cote; Page ITE-25 (top) © iStockphoto.com/MHJ.

We have made every effort to trace the ownership of all copyrighted material and to secure permission from copyright holders. In the event of any question arising as to the use of any material, we will be pleased to make the necessary corrections in future printings. Thanks are due to the aforementioned authors, publishers, and agents for permission to use the materials indicated.

ISBN: 978-0-76387-134-5 (print)
ISBN: 978-0-76386-678-5 (digital)

© 2017 by Paradigm Publishing, Inc.
875 Montreal Way
St. Paul, MN 55102
Email: educate@emcp.com
Website: ParadigmCollege.com

Printed in the United States of America

24 23 22 21 20 19 18 17   5 6 7 8 9 10 11 12

Microsoft Office

Brief Edition

Study Tools

Study tools include a presentation and a glossary. Use these resources to help you further develop skills learned in this section.

Knowledge Check

 Check your understanding by identifying concepts taught this section. If you are a SNAP user, launch the Knowledge Check from your Assignments page.

Recheck

 Check your understanding by taking this quiz. If you are a SNAP user, launch the Study Quiz from your Assignments page.

Microsoft® Word

Study Tools

Study tools include a presentation and In Brief step lists. Use these resources to help you further develop and review skills learned in this section.

Knowledge Check

SNAP Check your understanding by identifying application tools used in this section. If you are a SNAP user, launch the Knowledge Check from your Assignments page.

Recheck

SNAP Check your understanding by taking this quiz. If you are a SNAP user, launch the Recheck from your Assignments page.

Skills Exercise

SNAP Additional activities are available to SNAP users. If you are a SNAP user, access these activities from your Assignments page.

Skills Review

Data File

Review 1   Editing a Hawaiian Specials Document

1. Open **FCTHawaiianSpecials.docx** and then save it with the name **1-FCTHawaiianSpecials**.
2. Insert the word *spectacular* between the words *the* and *Pacific* in the first sentence below the *White Sands Charters* heading.
3. Move the insertion point to the beginning of the paragraph below the *Air Adventures* heading and then type the sentence Experience beautiful coastlines and magnificent waterfalls, and fly inside an active volcano.
4. Select and then delete the words *Depending on weather, marine conditions, and access, your* located in the third sentence in the paragraph below the *White Sands Charters* heading.
5. Capitalize the *g* in *guides*. (This word now begins the sentence.)
6. Select and then delete the last sentence in the *Air Adventures* section (the sentence that begins *View untouched areas from*).
7. Undo the deletion and then redo the deletion.
8. Move the insertion point to the beginning of the document and then complete a spelling and grammar check on the document. (*Molokini* is spelled correctly.)

9. Use Thesaurus to change *delightful* in the paragraph in the *White Sands Charter* section to *enchanting*.
10. Save **1-FCTHawaiianSpecials.docx**.

Review 2   Creating and Using an AutoCorrect Entry

1. With **1-FCTHawaiianSpecials.docx** open, display the AutoCorrect dialog box, type HA in the *Replace* text box, type Hawaiian in the *With* text box, click the Add button, and then close the dialog box. Close the Word Options dialog box.
2. Move the insertion point to the end of the document and then type the text shown in Figure WB-1.1.
3. Delete the HA AutoCorrect entry at the AutoCorrect dialog box.

Figure WB-1.1 Review 2, Step 2

Luau Legends

Enjoy a spectacular HA dinner show featuring lavish prime rib and authentic HA buffet. This uniquely HA experience includes a traditional lei greeting, exceptional food and beverages, magic music of the islands, and Hawaii's finest performers. Join us each evening beginning at 7:30 p.m. for an evening of delicious HA food and spectacular performances.

4. Save, print, and then close **1-FCTHawaiianSpecials.docx**.

Review 3   Editing an Agreement

Data File

1. Open **WEIncentiveAgt.docx** and then save it with the name **1-WEIncentiveAgt**.
2. Complete a spelling and grammar check on the document.
3. Search for all occurrences of *Employee* and replace them with *Carol Shepard*.
4. Search for all occurrences of *Company* and replace them with *Worldwide Enterprises*.
5. Save, print, and then close **1-WEIncentiveAgt.docx**.

Review 4   Preparing a Fax Sheet

1. Click the File tab and then click the *New* option.
2. At the New backstage area, click in the search text box, type equity fax, and then press the Enter key.
3. Click the *Fax (Equity theme)* template and then click the Create button.
4. Insert the following information in the specified location:

- To: Scott Drysdale
- From: (Type your first and last names.)
- Fax: (213) 555-3349
- Pages: 3

- Phone: (213) 555-3400
- Date: (Insert current date.)
- Re: Incentive Agreement
- CC: (Delete this placeholder.)

Insert a capital *X* in the *Please Reply* check box. Click the *[Type comments]* placeholder and then type the following comment: Please review the Incentive Agreement and then call me so we can schedule an appointment.
5. Save the document with the name **1-WEAgtFax**.
6. Print and then close the document.

Skills Assessment

Assessment 1 Editing a Letter

1. Open **PTMarqueeLtr.docx** and then save it with the name **1-PTMarqueeLtr**.
2. Move the insertion point a double space below the paragraph of text in the letter and then add the following information. (Write the information as a paragraph—do not use bullets.)
   - Costume research takes approximately two to three weeks.
   - If appropriate costumes cannot be found, costumes are sewn.
   - Anticipate five working days to sew a costume.
   - Include the number of costumes and approximate sizes.
   - A price estimate will be provided before costumes are purchased or sewn.
3. Use Thesaurus to replace *regarding* in the first sentence with an appropriate synonym.
4. Save, print, and then close **1-PTMarqueeLtr.docx**.

Assessment 2 Writing a Letter

1. Display the New backstage area, search for and download the Business letter (Median theme) template, and then use the following information to create the letter. (You determine the salutation and closing.)

   Sender's information:
   The Waterfront Bistro
   3104 Rivermist Drive
   Buffalo, NY 14280

   Recipient's information:
   Marquee Productions
   Mr. Josh Hart, Locations Director
   955 South Alameda Street
   Los Angeles, CA 90037

2. Write a letter as Dana Hirsch that covers the following points. (Write the information in paragraphs—do not use bullets.)
   - Explain that The Waterfront Bistro is a full-service catering company with a number of menus for breakfast, lunch, dinner, and morning and afternoon snacks. Include the price ranges for breakfast, lunch, dinner, and snack menus. (You determine the ranges.)
   - Offer a 5% discount if you cater for the duration of the filming.
   - Tell Mr. Hart that you would like to fax a variety of menu options to him.
   - Close the letter by telling him you are very interested in his business and say something positive about your catering service.
3. Save the completed letter document with the name **1-WBCateringLtr**.
4. Print and then close the document.

Assessment 3 Preparing a Fax

1. Display the New backstage area, search for and download the Fax (Equity theme) template, and then insert the necessary information in the specified fields. You are Dana Hirsch and you are sending the fax to Josh Hart (see information in Assessment 2). His fax number is (612) 555-2009 and his telephone number is (612) 555-2005. Insert an *X* in the *Please Comment* check box and indicate that the fax contains 11 pages.
2. Save the fax document with the name **1-WBFax**.
3. Print and then close the document.

Assessment 4   Finding Information on Changing Grammar Checking Options

1. Open **FCTNorwayTour.docx** and then save it with the name **1-FCTNorwayTour**.
2. Use the Help feature to learn how to show readability statistics and read information on understanding readability statistics (including the *Flesch* Reading Ease score and *Flesch-Kincaid* Grade Level score). After reading the information, display the Word Options dialog box (click the File tab and then click *Options*) with the *Proofing* option selected and then insert a check mark in the *Show readability statistics* check box.
3. Complete a spelling and grammar check on the document. (*Myrdal* and *Flesch* are spelled correctly.)
4. When the readability statistics display, make a note of the word count, the *Flesch* Reading Ease score and the *Flesch-Kincaid* Grade Level score. Type that information in the appropriate locations in **1-FCTNorwayTour.docx**.
5. Display the Word Options dialog box with the *Proofing* option selected, remove the check mark from the *Show readability statistics* check box, and then close the Word Options dialog box.
6. Save, print, and then close **1-FCTNorwayTour.docx**.

Assessment 5   Creating a Certificate

1. Display the New backstage area and then search for and download the Membership certificate template (If the Membership certificate template is not available, choose a similar certificate.)
2. Identify yourself as a member in good standing in the First Choice Travel Advantage Program.
3. Save the completed document and name it **1-Membership**.
4. Print and then close the document.

Marquee Challenge

Challenge 1   Preparing a Business Letter

1. Open **MPLtrhd.docx** and then save it with the name **1-MPLtrtoWB**.
2. Create the letter shown in Figure WB-1.2. (When you type the email address in the last paragraph and then press the spacebar, Word automatically converts it to a hyperlink [blue underlined text]. (To remove the hyperlink formatting, immediately click the Undo button.) Type your initials in place of the *XX* reference initials that displays toward the end of the document.)
3. Save, print, and then close **1-MPLtrtoWB.docx**.

Challenge 2   Editing and Formatting a Travel Document

1. Open **FCTRenoTahoeVac.docx** and then save it with the name **1-FCTRenoTahoeVac**.
2. Edit and format the document so it displays as shown in Figure WB-1.3 on page WB-8. (Search for all occurrences of *Eldorado* and replace with *Sierra*. Expand the Find and Replace dialog box, insert a check mark in the *Match case* check box, and then search for all occurrences of *LT* and replace with *Lake Tahoe*. Complete a spelling and grammar check on the document.)
3. Save, print, and then close **1-FCTRenoTahoeVac.docx**.

(**Current date**) *(press Enter three times)*

Ms. Dana Hirsch *(press Shift + Enter)*
The Waterfront Bistro *(press Shift + Enter)*
3104 Rivermist Drive *(press Shift + Enter)*
Buffalo, NY 14280 *(press Enter)*

Dear Ms. Hirsch: *(press Enter)*

We will be filming a movie in and around Toronto and Buffalo from July 18 to August 31, 2018. During that time, we will require catering services for cast and crew members. The services we request include breakfast, mid-morning snack, lunch, and afternoon snack for each day of filming, including weekends. *(press Enter)*

Please send information on your breakfast and lunch catering menus and snack choices. We are interested in pricing for meals and snacks for approximately 45 people for the duration of the filming. If you have any questions about our catering needs, please contact me by telephone at (612) 555-2005 or email me at JoshH@emcp.net. *(press Enter)*

Sincerely, *(press Enter two times)*

Josh Hart *(press Shift + Enter)*
Locations Director *(press Enter)*

XX *(press Shift + Enter)*
1-MPLtrtoWB.docx

955 South Alameda Street • Los Angeles, CA 90037
P: 612.555.2005 • F: 612.555.2009 • info@emcp.net • emcp.net/marquee

VACATIONING IN RENO AND LAKE TAHOE

Reno and Lake Tahoe are home to more snow, more ski resorts, and more nightlife than any other ski destination in North America. Come visit our area and experience a vast diversity of ski terrain, scenic beauty, and entertainment options. Getting to Reno and Lake Tahoe is as easy as taking one of over 250 flights that arrive daily at the Reno/Tahoe International Airport. Getting to your accommodations can be as quick as a ten-minute shuttle ride to a hotel casino in Reno or less than a scenic hour through the Sierra foothills to a variety of Lake Tahoe properties. All of the ski slopes are between 45 and 90 minutes from the Reno Airport. Getting around is easy with a variety of transportation options.

Destinations

Convenience and great locations make Incline Village and Crystal Bay desirable destinations at Lake Tahoe. Situated between Squaw Valley and Heavenly ski resorts, the two villages, along with other great resorts such as Mt. Rose and Diamond Peak, are just minutes away. Just 30 miles from Reno/Tahoe International Airport, the villages are central to all of the Lake Tahoe ski resorts. Diamond Peak offers 2,000 acres of classic Nordic terrain, over 35 kilometers of groomed tracks and skating lanes with incredible views of Lake Tahoe. The resort also boasts a 6.2-million-dollar complex including an eight-lane indoor swimming pool, cardiovascular and strength-training center, aerobic studio, and gym. Additional recreational offerings include sledding, sleigh rides, snowshoeing, bowling, and a movie theater.

North Lake Tahoe is a favored destination for discriminating vacationers. Visit this beautiful area for the epic powder, seven resorts, downhill and cross-country skiing, and unlimited dining choices—all for affordable prices. Consider trying ice skating at the world's highest ice rink, snowmobiling and snowshoeing in the backcountry, or touring Lake Tahoe on an authentic paddle-wheeler. Visit one of 80 restaurants boasting award-winning cuisine in lakeshore and alpine settings. Visit the historic town of Truckee, an old railroad and logging community with quaint shops and sights.

Lake Tahoe South Shore is the ideal destination for variety with an amazing selection of skiing for all skill levels. Almost endless lodging possibilities await you with over 95 luxurious hotels and casinos, all-suite resorts, motels, condominiums, cabins, and homes. Tour the Sierra backcountry on a snowmobile, take a paddle-wheeler cruise to Emerald Bay, try a peaceful sleigh ride, or see the sights from a dogsled.

Study Tools

Study tools include a presentation and In Brief step lists. Use these resources to help you further develop and review skills learned in this section.

Knowledge Check

SNAP Check your understanding by identifying application tools used in this section. If you are a SNAP user, launch the Knowledge Check from your Assignments page.

Recheck

SNAP Check your understanding by taking this quiz. If you are a SNAP user, launch the Recheck from your Assignments page.

Skills Exercise

SNAP Additional activities are available to SNAP users. If you are a SNAP user, access these activities from your Assignments page.

Skills Review

FIRST CHOICE
TRAVEL

Data File

Review 1   Applying Character Formatting to a Travel Document

1. Open **FCTPetersburg.docx** and then save it with the name **2-FCTPetersburg**.
2. Select the entire document, change the font to Cambria, the font size to 11 points, and the font color to Blue, Accent 5, Darker 50% (ninth column, bottom row in the *Theme Colors* section).
3. Set the title *PETERSBURG, ALASKA* in 16-point Corbel.
4. Set the heading *Services* in 14-point Corbel bold and then use Format Painter to apply the same formatting to the remaining headings (*Visitor Attractions*, *Walking Tours*, *Accommodations*, and *Transportation*).
5. Use the Font dialog box to apply small caps formatting to the last sentence in the document (the sentence that begins *If you would like more*).
6. Apply the Gradient Fill - Blue, Accent 5, Reflection text effect (second column, second row) to the title *PETERSBURG, ALASKA* and then apply bold formatting.
7. Save **2-FCTPetersburg.docx**.

 **Review 2** Applying Paragraph Formatting to a Travel Document

1. With **2-FCTPetersburg.docx** open, center the title *PETERSBURG, ALASKA*.
2. Justify the paragraph of text below the title *PETERSBURG, ALASKA*.
3. Center the last sentence in the document (the sentence that begins *IF YOU WOULD LIKE*).
4. Justify the two paragraphs of text below the *Services* heading and indent the text 0.5 inch from the left. (Apply the formatting to the blank lines following the paragraphs as well as the paragraphs.) Use Format Painter to apply the same formatting to the four paragraphs below the *Visitor Attractions* heading, the one paragraph below the *Walking Tours* heading, the two paragraphs below the *Accommodations* heading, and the two paragraphs below the *Transportation* heading.
5. Move the insertion point to the end of the document, press the Enter key two times, and then change the paragraph alignment to right alignment.
6. Type Melissa Gehring, press Shift + Enter, and then type First Choice Travel.
7. Select the entire document, change the line spacing to 1.15, and then deselect the document.
8. Click anywhere in the *Services* heading and then change the spacing after the paragraph to 6 points.
9. Use the Repeat command (F4) to insert 6 points of spacing after the remaining headings (*Visitor Attractions*, *Walking Tours*, *Accommodations*, and *Transportation*).
10. Save, print, and then close **2-FCTPetersburg.docx**.

 **Review 3** Applying Indent Formatting and Finding and Replacing Formatting in a Vacation Packages Document

Data File

1. Open **FCTVacPackages.docx** and then save it with the name **2-FCTVacPackages**.
2. Select the entire document and then change the line spacing to 1.0.
3. Select the four paragraphs of text below *Fast Facts* in the *OREGON* section, click the Decrease Indent button in the Paragraph group on the Home tab to remove the indent, and then insert bullets.
4. Select the four paragraphs of text below *Fast Facts* in the *NEVADA* section, click the Decrease Indent button to remove the indent, and then insert bullets.
5. Use the Find and Replace dialog box to search for all occurrences of text set in 11-point Calibri italic and replace them with 12-point Corbel bold italic.
6. Move the insertion point to the end of the document and then type the text shown in Figure WB-2.1. ***Hint: Insert the é, è, and ñ symbols with options at the Symbol dialog box with the Symbols tab selected and the* (normal text) *font selected.***
7. Save **2-FCTVacPackages.docx**.

Figure WB-2.1 Review 3, Step 6

Additional accommodations are available at the Ste. Thérèse Chateau and Silver Creek Resort. For information, please contact Carlos Nuñez.

Review 4 Creating Tabbed Text in a Vacation Packages Document

1. With **2-FCTVacPackages.docx** open, move the insertion point to the blank line below the heading *Rates and Packages* in the *OREGON* section and then set a left tab at the 1-inch mark on the horizontal ruler, a center tab at the 3.5-inch mark on the horizontal ruler, and a right tab at the 5.5-inch mark on the horizontal ruler.
2. Type the three bold column headings shown in Figure WB-2.2 (*Accommodations*, *No. Persons*, *Daily Price*).
3. Type the tabbed text shown in Figure WB-2.2.
4. Move the insertion point to the blank line below the heading *Rates and Packages* in the *NEVADA* section and then set a left tab at the 1-inch mark on the horizontal ruler, a center tab at the 3.5-inch mark on the horizontal ruler, and a right tab at the 5.5-inch mark on the horizontal ruler.
5. Type the three bold column headings shown in Figure WB-2.3 (*Package*, *Length*, and *Price*) and then press the Enter key.
6. Display the Tabs dialog box, add dot leaders to the tab set at the 3.5-inch mark and the tab set at the 5.5-inch mark, and then close the dialog box.
7. Type the text in columns below the headings as shown in Figure WB-2.3.
8. Save **2-FCTVacPackages.docx**.

Figure WB-2.2 Review 4, Steps 2–3

Accommodations	No. Persons	Daily Price
Studio/one bedroom	2 to 4	$75 to $125
Two bedrooms	4 to 6	$95 to $225
Three bedrooms	6 to 8	$135 to $300
Four bedrooms	8 to 12	$160 to $400
Five/six bedrooms	10 to 16	$250 to $500

Figure WB-2.3 Review 4, Steps 5 and 7

Package	Length	Price
Tuck 'n' Roll	3 days/2 nights	$269
Ski Sneak	4 days/3 nights	$409
Take a Break	6 days/5 nights	$649
Ultimate	8 days/7 nights	$1,009

Review 5 Applying Borders, Shading, Styles and Themes to a Vacation Packages Document

1. With **2-FCTVacPackages.docx** open, apply the Heading 1 style to the *OREGON* title and the *NEVADA* title.
2. Apply the Heading 2 style to the headings *Fast Facts* and *Rates and Packages* in the *OREGON* section and the *NEVADA* section.

3. Insert a bottom single-line border below the *OREGON* title and below the *NEVADA* title.
4. Apply a page border with the 3-D setting, the Blue, Accent 5, Darker 25% (ninth column, fifth row) color, and a 3-point width.
5. Apply the Basic (Simple) style set.
6. Apply the Frame theme.
7. Apply the Open paragraph spacing.
8. Select the tabbed text below the *Rates and Packages* heading in the *OREGON* section and apply Teal, Accent 5, Lighter 80% paragraph shading (ninth column, second row).
9. Select the tabbed text below the *Rates and Packages* heading in the *NEVADA* section and apply Teal, Accent 5, Lighter 80% paragraph shading.
10. Save, print, and then close **2-FCTVacPackages.docx.**

Skills Assessment

Assessment 1   Formatting a Cross-Country Skiing Document

1. Open **FCTLakeTahoeSkiing.docx** and then save it with the name **2-FCTLakeTahoeSkiing**.
2. Make the following changes to the document:
   a. Set the entire document in 12-point Constantia.
   b. Set the title in 14-point Calibri bold.
   c. Set the names of the cross-country skiing resorts in 14-point Calibri bold.
   d. Change the line spacing for the entire document to 1.3.
   e. Change the paragraph spacing after the title to 0 points.
   f. Change the paragraph spacing after each heading to 6 points.
   g. Indent one-half inch from the left margin and change the alignment to justify alignment for the paragraph of text below each cross-country skiing resort name.
   h. Center the title and apply Blue, Accent 1, Lighter 40% paragraph shading (fifth column, fourth row).
   i. Apply Blue, Accent 1, Lighter 80% paragraph shading (fifth column, second row) and insert a single-line bottom border to each cross-country skiing resort name.
   j. Insert a shadow page border in standard dark blue color that is 3 points in width.
   k. Apply the Integral theme.
3. Save, print, and then close **2-FCTLakeTahoeSkiing.docx**.

Assessment 2   Preparing and Formatting a Letter

1. Open **MPLtrhd.docx** and then save it with the name **2-MPLtrtoNPC**.
2. You are Neva Smith-Wilder, Educational Liaison for Marquee Productions. Write a letter using the date April 16, 2018, to Cal Rubine, Chair, Theatre Arts Division, Niagara Peninsula College, 2199 Victoria Street, Niagara-on-the-Lake, ON L0S 1J0 and include the following information:
   • Marquee Productions will be filming in and around the city of Toronto during the summer of 2018.

- Marquee Productions would like to use approximately 20 interns to assist with the shoot.
- Interns will perform a variety of tasks, including acting as extras, assisting the camera crew, working with set designers on set construction, and providing support to the production team.
- Interns can work approximately 15 to 30 hours per week and will be compensated at minimum wage.
- Close your letter by asking Mr. Rubine to screen interested students and then send approximately 20 names to you.
- If Mr. Rubine has any questions, he may contact you at (612) 555-2005 or send the names to you by email at NevaSW@emcp.net. (Word will automatically convert the email address to a hyperlink. To remove the hyperlink formatting, immediately click the Undo button.)

3. After typing the letter, apply the following formatting:
   a. Select the letter text and then change the font to Candara.
   b. Justify the paragraph(s) in the body of the letter.
4. Save, print, and then close **2-MPLtrtoNPC.docx**.

 **Assessment 3** Setting Leader Tabs

1. At a blank document, type the text shown in Figure WB-2.4 with the following specifications:
   a. Center, bold, and italicize the text as shown.
   b. Set the tabbed text as shown using a left tab for the first column and a right tab with leaders for the second column.
   c. After typing the text, select the entire document, change the font to Candara, and then change the spacing after paragraphs to 0 points.
2. Save the document and name it **2-WEDistSch**.
3. Print and then close **2-WEDistSch.docx**.

Figure WB-2.4 Assessment 3

WORLDWIDE ENTERPRISES

Distribution Schedule

Two by Two

United States ....May 4

Canada...June 15

Japan .... July 20

Australia/New Zealand .... August 3

Mexico...September 21

Assessment 4   Finding Information on Controlling Page Breaks

1. Use Word's Help feature to learn how to prevent page breaks between paragraphs and how to place at least two lines of a paragraph at the top or bottom of a page to prevent a widow (last line of a paragraph by itself at the top of a page) or orphan (first line of a paragraph by itself at the bottom of a page). (Consider reviewing the tutorial *Keeping Text Together* in Activity 2.4.)
2. Create a document containing the following information:
   a. Create a title for the document.
   b. Write a paragraph discussing how to prevent page breaks between paragraphs and list the steps required to complete the task.
   c. Write a paragraph discussing how to keep selected paragraphs together on a single page and list the steps required to complete the task.
   d. Write a paragraph discussing how to prevent a widow or orphan on a page in a document and list the steps required to complete the task.
3. Apply formatting to enhance the appearance of the document.
4. Save the completed document with the name **2-PageBreaks**.
5. Print and then close **2-PageBreaks.docx**.
6. Open **FCTVacSpecials.docx** and then save it with the name **2-FCTVacSpecials**.
7. Select the entire document and then change the font to 12-point Cambria.
8. Search for all occurrences of *Skye* and replace them with *Sky*.
9. Search for all occurrences of *Class* and replace them with *Category*.
10. Complete a spelling and grammar check on the document.
11. Click anywhere in the heading *Category S* (located toward the bottom of the first page) and then insert a command to keep the heading together with the next line.
12. Save the document and then print only page 2.
13. Close **2-FCTVacSpecials.docx**.

Assessment 5   Creating a Document with Tabbed Text

1. Determine a city outside of your state or province that you would like to visit. Using the Internet, identify four or more airlines that will fly from the airport nearest you to the city you would like to visit and determine the round-trip airfare.
2. Using the information you find, create a document with two tabbed columns. Set the first column as a left tab and type the name of the airline in this column. Set the second column as a right tab with leaders and type the airfare price in this column.
3. Create an appropriate heading for the tabbed text. Apply a paragraph border and/or shading to enhance the appearance of the tabbed text.
4. Apply a page border to the document.
5. Save the completed document with the name **2-Airfare**.
6. Print and then close **2-Airfare.docx**.

Marquee Challenge

Challenge 1   Editing and Formatting a Document on Juneau, Alaska

1. Open **FCTJuneau.docx** and then save it with the name **2-FCTJuneau**.
2. Apply the Heading 1 style to the title and the Heading 2 style to the headings.
3. Apply the Casual style set, change the theme colors to Green, change the theme fonts to Franklin Gothic, and apply the Open paragraph spacing. (Make these changes with buttons on the Design tab.)
4. Apply paragraph formatting and make changes so your document appears as shown in Figure WB-2.5.
5. Save, print, and then close **2-FCTJuneau.docx**.

Challenge 2   Creating and Formatting a Flier about a Skiing Vacation Package

1. Create the document shown in Figure WB-2.6. Apply the Cambria font, 1.5 line spacing, and page, border, shading, and bullet formatting as shown in the figure.
2. Save the completed document with the name **2-FCTSkiTahoe**.
3. Print and then close **2-FCTSkiTahoe.docx**.

JUNEAU, ALASKA

Juneau, Alaska's capital since 1900, sits at the base of Mt. Juneau. This capital blends its history as a mining town containing old storefronts and saloons with the modern architecture of government and Native corporations.

History

In the late 1800s, gold became the foundation of Juneau. The town contained a variety of gold mines with the Alaska-Juneau, or A-J, mine the most successful. The A-J mine buildings are still visible above town. Other gold mines include the Treadwill Mine complex at Douglas and the Alaska-Gastineau mine south of town. A massive cave-in occurred at Treadwill in 1917 and the mine closed. When gold content dropped below profitable margins in 1921, the Alaska-Gastineau mine closed. The A-J mine continued operations until World War II, when labor shortages and high costs forced its closure.

Visitor Attractions

Walking, hiking, and biking trails abound in and around the Juneau area. Scenic flights take visitors over the spectacular ice fields and the Glacier Bay National Monument. Take an exciting boat ride along Juneau's wilderness waterways. Tour buses take visitors to Mendanhall Glacier where they can climb moraines left by receding glaciers, hike nearby trails, and visit the U.S. Forest Service observatory where guides and exhibits explain glacier features. Visitors also can reach the glacier by driving or taking a charter flight.

Reminders of Juneau's past abound in the city. The Davis Log Cabin, built in 1881, was the community's first church and is now the visitor information center. Consider a visit to the St. Nicholas Russian Orthodox Church, which was built in 1894 and is considered the oldest original Orthodox Church in Southeast Alaska. Other city attractions include the Juneau Douglas City Museum, the pioneer cemetery, and the Wickersham House.

Museums

Juneau is the proud home to the Alaska State Museum, featuring permanent displays of Eskimo and Southeast Indian artifacts. The museum also offers changing displays of Alaska's political and natural history.

Visit the Juneau Douglas City Museum and learn about Juneau's history. Exhibits include features on gold mining and Juneau's historic past. A small admission fee is charged to adults. Children under the age of 18 are admitted free of charge.

The Alaska Maritime Heritage Foundation, a nonprofit group, is planning to build a tall ship for Alaska. It will be used to train sailors and people with disabilities in seamanship, environmental studies, goodwill trips, and charter work.

Ski Lake Tahoe

Super Value Ski Package®

Our exciting new Super Value Ski Package features special rates on a full line of top-quality resort and hotel rentals for three days or more. Ask for the Super Value Ski Package and receive a blizzard of valuable savings for one low, inclusive price. Whatever resort or hotel you choose, you will receive the following items for free or at a considerable discount.

- Receive one free adult day lift ticket and ski all day.
- If you would like to travel throughout the Lake Tahoe area, rent any vehicle and receive a 25% discount coupon.
- For your comfort and convenience, we will include a coupon for a free ski rack rental.
- Book a Super Value Ski Package by October 31 and receive four $25 gift certificates you can use at any of the fine dining restaurants in the area.

Accommodations

Resort	*3 to 5 Nights*	*7+ Nights*
Ambassador Inn	$699	$959
Hanover's at Lake Tahoe	$679	$929
Moore Creek Lodge	$629	$879
Evergreen Suites	$619	$859
St. Rémi Resort	$607	$837
Cedar Ridge Lodge	$547	$757
Mountain Lodge	$539	$729
River Creek Resort	$525	$715

Study Tools

Study tools include a presentation and In Brief step lists. Use these resources to help you further develop and review skills learned in this section.

Knowledge Check

 Check your understanding by identifying application tools used in this section. If you are a SNAP user, launch the Knowledge Check from your Assignments page.

Recheck

 Check your understanding by taking this quiz. If you are a SNAP user, launch the Recheck from your Assignments page.

Skills Exercise

SNAP Additional activities are available to SNAP users. If you are a SNAP user, access these activities from your Assignments page.

Skills Review

Review 1   Copying and Pasting Text Between Travel Documents

1. Open **FCTJuneauAK.docx** and then save it with the name **3-FCTJuneauAK**.
2. Select the entire document, click the *No Spacing* style in the Styles group, and then deselect the text.
3. Open **FCTJuneauInfo.docx**.
4. Display the Clipboard task pane and then make sure it is empty.
5. Select and then copy the text from the heading *Visitor Services* through the two paragraphs below the heading and the blank line below the two paragraphs.
6. Select and then copy the text from the heading *Transportation* through the paragraph below the heading and the blank line below the paragraph.
7. Select and then copy the text from the heading *Points of Interest* through the columns below the heading and the blank line below them.
8. Make **3-FCTJuneauAK.docx** the active document.
9. Display the Clipboard task pane.
10. Move the insertion point to the end of the document and then paste the text that begins with the heading *Points of Interest*.
11. Move the insertion point to the beginning of the heading *Points of Interest* and then paste the text that begins with the heading *Visitor Services*.

12. Move the insertion point to the beginning of the heading *Museums* and then paste the text that begins with the heading *Transportation*.
13. Clear the contents of the Clipboard task pane and then close the task pane.
14. Make **FCTJuneauInfo.docx** the active document and then close it.
15. Save **3-FCTJuneauAK.docx**.

Review 2 Moving and Formatting Text in a Travel Document

1. With **3-FCTJuneauAK.docx** open, select the heading *Visitor Centers*, the three paragraphs of text below it, and the blank line below them, and then move the selected text before the heading *Visitor Attractions*.
2. Select the heading *Museums*, the three paragraphs of text below it, and the blank line below the three paragraphs, and then move the selected text before the heading *Visitor Attractions*.
3. Change the top and bottom margins to 1.25 inches and the left and right margins to 1 inch.
4. Apply the Heading 1 style to the title *JUNEAU, ALASKA* and apply the Heading 2 style to the headings in the document (*History*, *Visitor Centers*, *Museums*, *Visitor Attractions*, *Transportation*, *Visitor Services*, and *Points of Interest*).
5. Apply the Lines (Stylish) style set, apply the Banded theme, and change the colors to *Blue II*.
6. Insert the Plain Number 3 page numbering style that inserts the page number in the upper right corner of each page.
7. Insert the SAMPLE 1 watermark.
8. Save, print, and then close **3-FCTJuneauAK.docx**.

Review 3 Formatting a Report in MLA Style

1. Open **PTRenaissanceRpt.docx** and then save it with the name **3-PTRenaissanceRpt**.
2. Select the entire document, change the font to 12-point Cambria, change the line spacing to double line spacing, and then remove the spacing after paragraphs.
3. Move the insertion point to the beginning of the document, type your name, press the Enter key, type your instructor's name, press the Enter key, type the title of your course, press the Enter key, and then type the current date.
4. Insert a header that displays your last name and the page number at the right margin and changes the font to 12-point Cambria. (For help, refer to Steps 11–15 in Activity 3.7.)
5. Make sure MLA style is selected in the Citations & Bibliography group on the References tab.
6. Position the insertion point after the word *century* (but before the period) in the last sentence of the first paragraph and then insert the source information from a journal article using the following information:
   Author = Marcus Gerard
   Title = History of the Renaissance Period
   Journal Name = European History: Early Modern Europe
   Year = 2018
   Pages = 13-17

7. Position the insertion point after the text *1494* (but before the period) in the first sentence in the third paragraph and then insert the source information from a book using the following information:

   Author = Iris Brooke
   Title = A History of Renaissance Costumes
   Year = 2017
   City = New York
   Publisher = Hudson River Publishing House

8. Insert a works cited page as a new page at the end of the document.
9. Edit the Gerard source so the journal name displays as *European History: Western European Civilization.*
10. Update the works cited page.
11. Format the works cited page to MLA standards by making the following changes (for help, refer to Steps 10–13 in Activity 3.8):
    a. Select the *Works Cited* heading and all entries, click the *No Spacing* style, change the font to 12-point Cambria, and change the line spacing to double line spacing.
    b. Center the title *Works Cited.*
    c. Hang-indent the entries.
12. Save, print, and then close **3-PTRenaissanceRpt.docx.**

Review 4   Preparing and Formatting an Announcement

1. At a blank document, use the Click and Type feature to type the text shown in Figure WB-3.1. ***Hint: Press Shift + Enter after typing* Sponsored by.**
2. Select the centered text you just typed and then change the font to 14-point Candara bold.
3. Select the right-aligned text you just typed and then change the font to 10-point Candara bold.
4. Change the vertical alignment of the text on the page to center alignment.
5. Save the document and name it **3-MPEmpOpps01.**
6. Print **3-MPEmpOpps01.docx.**
7. Save the document with the name **3-MPEmpOpps02.**
8. Change the vertical alignment of the text on the page back to top alignment.
9. Using the Online Pictures button, insert an image from the Internet related to movies. You determine the image as well as its size and position.
10. Delete the text *Marquee Productions* from the document and then use the Pictures button to insert the Marquee Productions logo image **MPLogo.jpg** below the text *Sponsored by.* Adjust the size and position of the image so it displays below *Sponsored by* and is approximately 0.9 inches wide.
11. Save, print, and then close **3-MPEmpOpps02.docx.**

Figure WB-3.1 Review 4

EMPLOYMENT OPPORTUNITIES

Working in the Movie Industry

Wednesday, March 14, 2018

7:00 to 8:30 p.m.

Sponsored by
Marquee Productions

Review 5   Preparing an Envelope

1. At a blank document, prepare an envelope with the return address and delivery address shown below. (Type your name below *First Choice Travel* in the return address.) Add the envelope to the document.

   Delivery address: Return address:

   Chris Greenbaum   First Choice Travel
   Marquee Productions   Student Name
   955 South Alameda Street   3588 Ventura Boulevard
   Los Angeles, CA 90037   Los Angeles, CA 90102

2. Save the document and name it **3-FCTEnv**.
3. Print and then close **3-FCTEnv.docx**. (Manual feed of the envelope may be required.)

Review 6   Preparing Mailing Labels

1. At a blank document, prepare a sheet of mailing labels for the following name and address using the Avery US Letter vendor and 5160 Easy Peel Address Labels product number. (Type your name below *Worldwide Enterprises*.)

   Worldwide Enterprises
   Student Name
   1112-1583 Broadway
   New York, NY 10110

2. Save the mailing label document and name it **3-WELabels**.
3. Print and then close **3-WELabels.docx**.

Skills Assessment

Assessment 1   Formatting a Costume Rental Agreement

1. Open **PTAgreement.docx** and then save it with the name **3-PTAgreement**.
2. Search for all occurrences of *Customer* and replace them with *Marquee Productions*.
3. Move the *4. Alterations* section above the *3. Marquee Productions Agrees* section and then renumber the two sections.

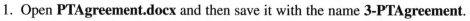

4. Select the entire document, change the font to 12-point Constantia, and then deselect the document.
5. Change the top margin to 1.5 inches.
6. Insert the Semaphore footer.
7. Save, print, and then close **3-PTAgreement.docx**.

Assessment 2   Creating an Announcement

1. At a blank document, create an announcement for Niagara Peninsula College by typing the text shown in Figure WB-3.2.
2. Change the font for the entire document to a decorative font, size, and color of your choosing.
3. Change the line spacing to double line spacing for the entire document.
4. Insert, size, and move an online image of your choosing related to the subject of the announcement.
5. Save the document and name it **3-NPCInternship**.
6. Print and then close **3-NPCInternship.docx**.

Figure WB-3.2 Assessment 2

NIAGARA PENINSULA COLLEGE

Internship Opportunities

June 18 through August 31, 2018

Marquee Productions, Toronto Office

Contact Cal Rubine, Theatre Arts Division

Assessment 3   Preparing Mailing Labels

1. Prepare return mailing labels with the following information. (Type your name below *Niagara Peninsula College*.)

    Niagara Peninsula College
    Student Name
    2199 Victoria Street
    Niagara-on-the-Lake, ON L0S 1J0

2. Save the labels document and name it **3-NPCLabels**.
3. Print and then close **3-NPCLabels.docx**.

Assessment 4   Finding Information on Creating a Picture Watermark

1. Open **3-MPEmpOpps01.docx** and save it with the name **3-MPEmpOpps-Wtrmark**.
2. Use Word's Help feature to learn how to insert a picture watermark.
3. Insert **MPLogo.jpg**, as a watermark.
4. Save, print, and then close **3-MPEmpOpps-Wtrmark.docx**.

Assessment 5   Creating a Personal Letterhead

1. At a blank document, create a letterhead that includes your first and last names, address, and telephone number, and insert an image in the letterhead that represents you or something in which you are interested. Apply font formatting to the text in the letterhead and size and position the image. (For letterhead examples, refer to **FCTLtrhd.docx** and **MPLtrhd.docx**. The letterheads in these two documents were created as headers. If you want to create your letterhead in a header, click the Insert tab, click the Header button in the Header & Footer group and then click *Edit Header*.)
2. Save the document and name it **3-Ltrhd**.
3. Print and then close **3-Ltrhd.docx**.

Marquee Challenge

Challenge 1   Formatting a Costume Document

1. Open **PTCostumes.docx** and then save it with the name **3-PTCostumes**.
2. Format your document so it displays similar to the document in Figure WB-3.3 on pages WB-25–WB-26. To do this, apply the following formatting:
   * Change the top margin to *1.25"*.
   * Insert, size, and position **PTLogo.jpg** as shown. *Hint: Change the position to* **Position in Top Center with Square Text Wrapping** *and then change the text wrapping to* **Top and Bottom.**
   * Apply the Heading 1 style to the headings.
   * Apply the Lines (Simple) style set.
   * Apply the Ion theme and then apply the Candara theme font. (Use the Fonts button on the Design tab.)
   * Apply bold and italic formatting to the headings.
   * Apply White, Background 1, Darker 5% paragraph shading to the headings (first column, second row).
   * Insert the page border (the tenth page border option from the end of the *Art* option drop-down list) and then change the width to 6 points and the color to standard dark red (in the *Standard Colors* section).
   * Change the paragraph alignment and insert numbers and bullets as shown.
   * Insert **Books.png**. Change the image color to Dark Red, Accent color 1 Light (second column, third row in the *Recolor* section), the correction to Brightness: +40% Contrast: +40% (last option in the *Brightness/Contrast* section) and then size and position the image as shown.
3. Save, print, and then close **3-PTCostumes.docx**.

Worldwide Enterprises   Challenge 2   Preparing an Announcement

1. At a blank document, create the document shown in Figure WB-3.4 on page WB-27 with the following specifications:
   * Apply the No Spacing style.
   * Change the line spacing to 1.5 lines and change the font size to 16 points.
   * Change to landscape orientation.
   * Press the Enter key three times and then type the text in the document. When typing the text, press the Enter key after typing the title and press Shift + Enter to end each remaining line of text. *Note: Do not press the Enter key or Shift + Enter after the last line.*

- Apply the page border and insert the page background color as shown in the figure.
- Insert **WELogo.jpg**. Change the white background of the logo image to transparent by clicking the Color button on the Picture Tools Format tab, clicking the *Set Transparent Color* option, and then clicking in a white area inside the logo image. Size and position the image as shown in the figure.
- Insert **Businesspeople.png**. Set the white background of the image to transparent color. Size and position the image as shown in the figure.
- Insert the watermark as shown.

2. Save the document and name it **3-WENotice**.
3. Print and then close **3-WENotice.docx**.

Figure WB-3.3 Challenge 1

Renaissance Period

The Renaissance period was a series of cultural and literary movements that took place in the fourteenth, fifteenth, and sixteenth centuries in Europe. The word *renaissance* means "rebirth" and originated with the belief that Europeans had rediscovered the intellectual and cultural superiority of the Greek and Roman cultures. The Renaissance period was preceded by the Middle Ages, also known as the "Dark Ages," which began with the collapse of the Roman Empire in the fifth century. The term *renaissance* was coined by Jacob Burckhardt in the eighteenth century in *The Civilization of the Renaissance in Italy*.

Renaissance education was designed to produce a person well-versed in humanities, mathematics, science, sports, and art. The Renaissance person had extensive knowledge in many fields, explored beyond the boundaries of learning and geographical knowledge, and embraced free thought and skepticism. Artists, writers, explorers, architects, and scientists were motivated by a revival in classical Greek and Roman culture and a return to classical values. During the Middle Ages, interest in culture and learning was primarily confined to theologians, philosophers, and writers. During the Renaissance period, however, people from all social, political, and economic classes involved themselves in the study of classical literature and art.

Renaissance Costume

Renaissance costume developed in Italy and was introduced to Western Europe following the invasion of Italy by Charles VIII of France in 1494. Due to the warmer climate in Italy, simpler styles evolved independently from the rest of Europe. Men's clothing consisted of low-necked tunics and chemises and women's clothing consisted of simple and low-necked gowns called "Juliet" gowns. During the middle of the fifteenth century, clothing assumed a more natural appearance. Women wore dresses with attached bodices and skirts. Men's doublets became shorter and hosiery became more prominent. Interest by women in gothic headdresses declined and instead they trimmed their hair with veils, ribbons, and jewels. Lace and perfume became more prevalent during the Renaissance period.

Early in the Renaissance period, women's dress included a long, rigid, cone-shaped corset reaching below the waist to a "V" in the front. Women's gowns expanded below the waistline and by the middle sixteenth century were supported by hoops made of wire that were held together with ribbons. This hoop skirt, called a *farthingale*, reached its maximum width around the early seventeenth century and then changed to a cartwheel or drum shape. Ballooned sleeves and circular lace collars also typified the early seventeenth century costume. Men's clothing had a similar look with puffed-out hose, balloon sleeves, padded doublets, and large ruff collars.

continues

Costume Vocabulary

1. Basquine: A very large skirt that was open and stretched on circles.
2. Berne: A very large, fixed, and pleated scarf that rested on the shoulder.
3. Jupon: Long-sleeved camisole generally worn by men and women in Spain.
4. Mantilla: A kind of shawl worn by women to cover the head and shoulders.
5. Marlotte: A coat with pleats in the back and short, curved sleeves.

Costume Books

- Arnold, Janet, *Patterns of Fashion*
- Barton, Lucy, *Historic Costume for the Stage*
- Boucher, Francois, *20,000 Years of Fashion*
- Brooke, Iris, *A History of Costume*
- Evans, Mary, *Costume Throughout the Ages*
- LaMar, Virginia A., *English Dress in the Age of Shakespeare*

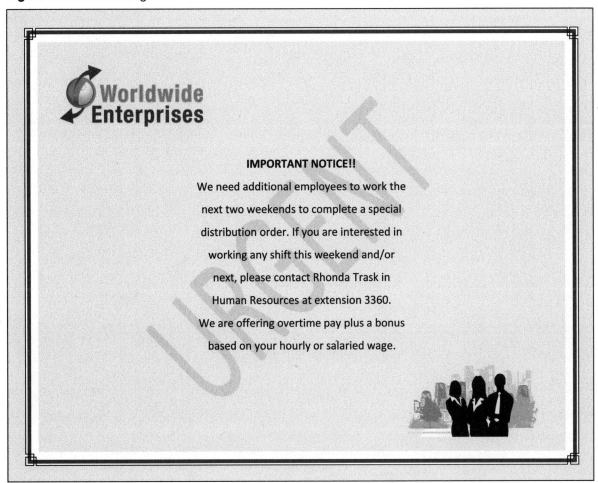

IMPORTANT NOTICE!!

We need additional employees to work the next two weekends to complete a special distribution order. If you are interested in working any shift this weekend and/or next, please contact Rhonda Trask in Human Resources at extension 3360. We are offering overtime pay plus a bonus based on your hourly or salaried wage.

Microsoft® Excel®

Study tools include a presentation and In Brief step lists. Use these resources to help you further develop and review skills learned in this section.

SNAP Check your understanding by identifying application tools used in this section. If you are a SNAP user, launch the Knowledge Check from your Assignments page.

Recheck

SNAP Check your understanding by taking this quiz. If you are a SNAP user, launch the Recheck from your Assignments page.

Skills Exercise

SNAP Additional activities are available to SNAP users. If you are a SNAP user, access these activities from your Assignments page.

Skills Review

Note: If you submit your work in hard copy, check with your instructor before completing these reviews to find out if you need to print two copies of each worksheet with one of the copies showing formulas in cells instead of the calculated results.

Data File

Review 1   Entering Labels, Values, and Formulas

1. Open **WBQtrlyIncome.xlsx** and then save it with the name **1-WBQtrlyIncome**.
2. Type Jul in cell B4.
3. Use the fill handle in cell B4 to enter sequential monthly labels in cells C4 and D4.
4. Type 1300 in cell B11.
5. Use the fill handle in cell B11 to copy the same value to cells C11 and D11.
6. Click in cell B12 and then use the AutoSum button to enter a formula that adds the range B9:B11.
7. Copy the formula in cell B12 to cells C12 and D12.
8. Click in cell B14 and then enter a formula that subtracts the total expenses from gross margin by typing =b7-b12.
9. Copy the formula in cell B14 to cells C14 and D14.
10. Click in cell B15 and then enter a formula that multiplies the net income before taxes by taxes of 22% by typing =b14*.22.
11. Copy the formula in cell B15 to cells C15 and D15.

12. Click in cell B16 and then enter a formula that subtracts the taxes from net income before taxes by typing =b14-b15.
13. Copy the formula in cell B16 to cells C16 and D16.
14. Save **1-WBQtrlyIncome.xlsx**.

Review 2   Improving the Appearance of the Worksheet; Previewing and Printing

1. With **1-WBQtrlyIncome.xlsx** open, merge and center the title in row 1 across columns A through D.
2. Merge and center the text in row 2 across columns A through D.
3. Merge and center the text in row 3 across columns A through D.
4. Change the alignment of the range B4:D4 to right alignment.
5. Apply the Accounting format to the range B5:D16.
6. Display the worksheet in the Print backstage area to preview how the worksheet will look when printed and then print the worksheet. *Note: If necessary, AutoFit the columns so that all of the data is visible.*
7. Display formulas in the worksheet cells and then print another copy of the worksheet.
8. Turn off the display of formulas in the worksheet.
9. Save and then close **1-WBQtrlyIncome.xlsx**.

Skills Assessment

Note: If you submit your work in hard copy, check with your instructor before completing these assessments to find out if you need to print two copies of each worksheet with one of the copies showing the formulas in cells instead of the calculated results.

Assessment 1   Creating a New Workbook

1. Open Excel and then open a blank workbook.
2. Enter the labels and data in the image in Figure WB-1.1 using the following instructions:
   a. Enter the titles in cells A1 and A2 and then merge and center the ranges A1:G1 and A2:G2.
   b. Enter the labels in column A and then AutoFit column A by double-clicking the boundary between the column A and column B headings.
   c. Enter the remaining labels and data using the fill handle to enter repetitive or series data. (Type the percentage sign after the number *85* in column F.)
3. Enter the following formulas in the worksheet:
   a. Enter a SUM function in cell E4 that totals the values in the range B4:D4 and then use the fill handle to copy the formula into cell E9.
   b. Enter a SUM function in cell B10 that totals the values in the range B4:B9 and then use the fill handle to copy the formula into cell E10.
   c. Enter a formula in G4 that multiplies the subtotal in cell E4 by the exchange rate in cell F4 and then copy the formula into cell G10.
4. Apply the Accounting format to the appropriate cells.

5. Apply alignment and font formatting options you learned in this section as needed to improve the appearance of the worksheet.
6. AutoFit columns that do not display the full contents of the cells.
7. Save the workbook with the name **1-MPExpenses**.
8. Preview the worksheet, change to landscape orientation, and then print the worksheet.
9. Close **1-MPExpenses.xlsx**.

Figure WB-1.1 Assessment 1

	A	B	C	D	E	F	G
1	Marquee Productions						
2	Filming Expenses July - September 2018						
3		Jul	Aug	Sep	Subtotal	Exchange Rate	Total
4	Actors/Actresses	22000	24500	20150		85%	
5	AV Equipment	16050	16050	16050		85%	
6	Costume Rental	8900	8900	8900		85%	
7	Catering	3950	4850	3700		85%	
8	Location Fees	12050	12050	12050		85%	
9	Transportation	5500	5900	5700		85%	
10	Total					85%	
11							

Assessment 2 Entering Formulas and Editing Data

Data File

1. Open **FCTSales.xlsx** and then save it with the name **1-FCTSales**.
2. Enter a SUM function in cell F4 that sums the four quarter sales figures for Jonas Arund.
3. Use the fill handle to copy the formula in cell F4 down into cell F9.
4. Enter a formula in cell G4 that multiplies the total sales (cell F4) by a 9% commission for Jonas Arund. *Hint: Type the commission percent as **.09.***
5. Use the fill handle to copy the formula in cell G4 down into cell G9.
6. Make cell A8 active and then edit the last name so it does not include the *s* (it should read *Frank*).
7. Make cell C8 active and then replace the cell contents with the value *34541*.
8. Make cell E7 active and then replace the cell contents with the value *29848*.
9. Undo the last action.
10. Apply alignment and formatting options you learned in this section as needed to improve the appearance of the worksheet.
11. Save, print, and then close **1-FCTSales.xlsx**.

Assessment 3 Creating a New Workbook

1. Open Excel and then create a new workbook that tracks how many First Choice Travel bookings are made for various cities, the average sale price for each city, and a total sales estimate for each city using the following instructions:
   a. Enter the company name, *First Choice Travel*, in the first row and a title for the worksheet in the second row.
   b. Enter the labels and values in Table WB-1.1, starting with the label City in cell A3.
   c. Enter the label Total Sales Estimate in cell D3 with a manual line break inserted between the words Sales and Estimate.
2. Enter a formula in cell D4 that multiplies the bookings by the average sale price.

Table WB-1.1 Assessment 3

City	Bookings	Average Sale Price
New York	89	3890
Tucson	23	2785
Los Angeles	104	3740
Denver	36	2610
Orlando	62	3170
Des Moines	9	1925
Wichita	8	2100
Boston	41	3170
Philadelphia	21	1970
Dallas	56	2435
Milwaukee	13	2615
Atlanta	40	2690
Vancouver	37	3420
Calgary	28	3295
Toronto	23	2855
Montreal	38	2660

3. Use the fill handle to copy the formula through cell D19.
4. Apply alignment and formatting options you learned in this section as needed to improve the appearance of the worksheet.
5. Use the Tell Me feature to change the font color for the company name in cell A1 to standard blue.
6. Save the workbook with the name **1-FCTCities**.
7. Turn on the display of formulas.
8. Print and then close **1-FCTCities.xlsx**.

 **Worldwide Enterprises**

Data File

Assessment 4 Finding Information on Number Formatting

1. In Activity 1.9, you learned how to apply the Accounting format. Other number formats are available for different purposes. Use the Tell Me feature or Excel Help feature to find out how to apply the Comma and Percentage number formats to cells and decrease the amount of digits that display after the decimal point.
2. Open **WEBudget.xlsx** and then save it with the name **1-WEBudget**.
3. Apply the Comma format (using the Comma Style button) to the range B5:C15 and remove any digits that display after the decimal point.
4. Apply the Percentage format (using the Percent Style button) to the range D4:D17.
5. Print the worksheet.
6. Save and then close **1-WEBudget.xlsx**.

INDIVIDUAL CHALLENGE

Assessment 5 Creating a School Budget

1. Create a worksheet to calculate the estimated total cost of completing your diploma or certificate. You determine the items that need to be included in the worksheet, such as tuition, fees, textbooks, supplies, accommodation costs, transportation, telephone, food, and entertainment. If necessary, use the Internet to find reasonable cost estimates if you want to include an item such as cell phone charges and want to research competitive rates for your area. Arrange the labels and values by quarter,

semester, or academic year according to your preference. Make sure to include a total that shows the total cost of your education.

2. Save the workbook with the name **1-SchoolBudget**.
3. Apply alignment and formatting options you learned in this section as needed to improve the appearance of the worksheet.
4. If necessary, change to landscape orientation and then print the worksheet.
5. Save and then close **1-SchoolBudget.xlsx**.

Marquee Challenge

Challenge 1   Preparing an International Student Registration Report

1. You work at Niagara Peninsula College in the Registrar's Office. The Registrar has asked you to create the annual report for international student registrations. Create the worksheet shown in Figure WB-1.2.
2. Calculate the tuition fees in column I by multiplying the credit hours times the fee per hour and then use the SUM function to calculate the total international student fees.
3. Apply format options as shown and apply the Accounting format to the amounts in columns H and I.
4. Add the current date and your name in rows 4 and 18, respectively.
5. Change to landscape orientation.
6. Save the workbook with the name **1-NPCIntlRegRpt**.
7. Print and then close **1-NPCIntlRegRpt.xlsx**.

Figure WB-1.2 Challenge 1

	A	B	C	D	E	F	G	H	I
1				Niagara Peninsula College					
2				International Student Registrations					
3				for the 2018/2019 Academic Year					
4				Report Date: Current Date					
5	ID #	Last Name	First Name	Home Country	Program	Semester	Credit Hours	Fee per Hour	Tuition Fee
6	241588	Cano	Sergio	Spain	BIS11	1	45	432	
7	241578	Flannigan	Maren	Ireland	BIS11	1	60	432	
8	241856	Chou	Terry	China	BMK12	1	45	432	
9	286953	Zhang	Joseph	China	BIN32	2	45	432	
10	274586	Alivero	Maria	Mexico	CMP12	2	45	432	
11	268451	Torres	Phillip	Ecuador	CTN14	2	60	432	
12	234851	Davis	Caitlyn	Australia	OAM24	3	60	432	
13	299635	Muir	Christa	Australia	GRD13	4	30	432	
14	247523	North	Marlo	Bahamas	HTC24	2	30	432	
15	277458	Cervinka	Mary	Croatia	TTM14	4	30	432	
16									
17					TOTAL INTERNATIONAL STUDENT FEES:				
18	Prepared by: Student Name								
19									

Challenge 2   Preparing a Theatre Arts Target Enrollment Report

1. You work with Cal Rubine, chair of the Theatre Arts Division at Niagara Peninsula College. Cal needs the target student enrollment report to assist with the revenue projections for the upcoming budget. Cal has asked you to create the worksheet shown in Figure WB-1.3.

Figure WB-1.3 Challenge 2

	A	B	C	D	E	F
1	Niagara Peninsula College					
2	Theatre Arts Division					
3	Target Student Enrollments					
4	for the 2018/2019 Academic Year					
5						
6	Academic chair: Cal Rubine					
7						
8	Program Name	Program Code	Semester Offering	Target Percent	Actual Enrollment 2017/2018	Target Enrollment
9	Theatre Arts: Acting	TAA12	1 2 3 4		210	
10	Theatre Arts: Stage Management	TAM23	1 2		55	
11	Theatre Arts: Lighting & Effects	TAL42	1 2		67	
12	Theatre Arts: Production	TAP32	1 2 3 4		221	
13	Theatre Arts: Sound	TAS14	1 2		38	
14	Theatre Arts: Businsess Management	TAB25	1 2 3 4		64	
15						
16			ESTIMATED ENROLLMENTS FOR 2018/2019:			
17						
18	Report date: Current Date					
19	Prepared by: Student Name					
20						

2. Cal uses the actual enrollments from the prior year (2017/2018) to calculate the target for the next year. In some programs, Cal expects that enrollment will be higher than the previous year due to new registrants, transfers from other programs, and students returning to pick up missed credits. In other programs, Cal expects that enrollment will decline from the previous year due to students dropping the program, transferring to other colleges, and failing to meet the minimum GPA for progression. Cal has provided the percentages in Table WB-1.2 for you to use to create the formulas in the *Target Percent* column. Insert the target percent in the worksheet and then enter a formula in column F to determine the target enrollment.
3. Use the SUM function in cell F16 to calculate the total estimated enrollments.
4. Autofit columns A, E, and F.
5. Apply alignment options as shown and add the current date and your name in rows 18 and 19, respectively.
6. If necessary, format the values in the *Target Percent* column to zero digits past the decimal point and the values in the *Target Enrollment* column to two digits past the decimal point.
7. Change to landscape orientation.
8. Save the workbook with the name **1-NPCTargetEnrolRpt**.
9. Print and then close **1-NPCTargetEnrolRpt.xlsx**.

Table WB-1.2 Challenge 2

Program Name	Target Percent
Theatre Arts: Acting	95%
Theatre Arts: Stage Management	106%
Theatre Arts: Lighting & Effects	112%
Theatre Arts: Production	85%
Theatre Arts: Sound	103%
Theatre Arts: Business Management	75%

Study Tools

SNAP Study tools include a presentation and In Brief step lists. Use these resources to help you further develop and review skills learned in this section.

Knowledge Check

SNAP Check your understanding by identifying application tools used in this section. If you are a SNAP user, launch the Knowledge Check from your Assignments page.

Recheck

SNAP Check your understanding by taking this quiz. If you are a SNAP user, launch the Recheck from your Assignments page.

Skills Exercise

SNAP Additional activities are available to SNAP users. If you are a SNAP user, access these activities from your Assignments page.

Skills Review

The Waterfront
B|STRO

Review 1   Editing, Moving, Copying, and Clearing Cells; Performing a Spell Check; Inserting and Deleting Rows

Data File

1. Open **WBInvToNPC.xlsx** and save it with the name **2-WBInvToNPC**.
2. Change the amount in cell D20 from *13.73* to *15.23*.
3. Clear the contents of cell A8.
4. Change the label in cell A21 from *Soup* to *French Onion Soup*.
5. Type new data in the cells indicated.
   E14   PO No.   F14   TA-11-643
6. Delete rows 7, 8, and 9.
7. Complete a spelling check of the worksheet. (All names are spelled correctly.)
8. Move the range E7:F7 to E10:F10.
9. Copy cell A24 to cell A30.
10. Delete the rows that contain the labels *Milk* and *Donuts*.
11. Insert a new row between *Prime Rib* and *Mixed Vegetables* and then type Seafood Pasta in column A of the new row.
12. Save **2-WBInvToNPC.xlsx**.

Review 2   Adjusting Column Widths; Replacing Data; Moving Cells

1. With **2-WBInvToNPC.xlsx** open, adjust the width of column A to 17.00 characters.
2. Change the width of column C to the length of the longest entry (AutoFit).
3. Change the width of column D to 17.00 characters and column E to 7.00 characters.
4. Use the Replace feature to replace the value *32* with *36* for all occurrences.
5. Create a SUM formula in cell F33 to total cells F17 through F31.
6. Apply numeric formats as follows:
   a. Apply the Accounting format to cells F17 and F33.
   b. Apply the Comma format (using the Comma Style button) to cells F28 and F31.
7. Indent one time the ranges A18:A27 and A29:A30.
8. Select the range D1:D3 and then change the font to 10-point Cambria bold.
9. Move the range D1:D3 to F1:F3 and then align the text at the right edge of the cells.
10. Save **2-WBInvToNPC.xlsx**.

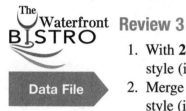

Review 3   Applying Formatting Features; Inserting an Image

1. With **2-WBInvToNPC.xlsx** open, merge and center and then apply the Input cell style (in the *Data and Model* section) to the range A17:B17 and A28:B28.
2. Merge and center cell A5 across columns A through F and then apply the Title cell style (in the *Titles and Headings* section) to cell A5.
3. Center the values in columns C and D and the labels in the range C16:F16.
4. Add a top and bottom border to the range A16:F16 and apply bold formatting.
5. Add a top and double bottom border to cell F33 and apply bold formatting.
6. Add an outside border to the range A1:F36.
7. Add the fill color Green, Accent 6, Lighter 80% (last column, second row in *Theme Colors* section) to cell A5.
8. Add the fill color Green, Accent 6, Lighter 60% (last column, third row in the *Theme Colors* section) to the range A16:F16.
9. Apply the Integral theme to the worksheet.
10. Apply the Green Yellow theme colors.
11. Make cell A1 the active cell and then insert the image **TWBLogo.jpg**.
12. Change the height of the image to 0.75 inch.
13. Save, print, and then close **2-WBInvToNPC.xlsx**.

Skills Assessment

Note: If you submit your work in hard copy, check with your instructor before completing these Assessments to find out if you need to print two copies of each worksheet, with one of the copies showing the cell formulas instead of the calculated results.

Assessment 1   Editing Cells; Inserting Columns; Copying Formulas; Inserting Images; Applying Formatting Features

1. Open **PTMarqCost.xlsx** and save it with the name **2-PTMarqCost**.
2. Complete the worksheet using the following information:
   a. Design costs for all costumes should display as *122.50* instead of *22*.

b. Insert a new column between *Fabric* and *Total Cost* and type the column heading *Notions* in cell I3. Type the values in the range I4:I10 as follows:

Henry II	101.50	John	47.85
Queen Eleanor	88.23	Geoffrey	47.85
Alias	58.40	Philip	47.85
Richard	47.85		

   c. The formula to calculate total cost for each costume is incorrect. Enter the correct formula for the first costume (cell J4) and then copy the formula to the range J5:J10. *Hint: The current formula does not include the fabric and notions costs. Add the correct cells to the end of the formula.*

   d. Create a formula in cell K4 to calculate the costume fee that will multiply the total cost in cell J4 by 1.5 and then copy the formula to the range K5:K10.

   e. Create a formula in cell L4 to calculate the profit as costume fee minus total cost and then copy the formula to the range L5:L10.

   f. Format the numeric cells in an appropriate style.

   g. Change the alignment of any headings that could be improved in appearance.

   h. Merge and center the titles in cells A1 and A2 over columns A to L.

   i. Adjust the height of row 1 to 54.00 points and row 2 to 30.00 points.

   j. Insert the image **PTLogo.jpg** and then resize it to fit in the top row at the top left of the worksheet.

   k. Apply font, border, and color changes to enhance the appearance of the worksheet. Adjust column widths as needed.

   l. Change to landscape orientation.

3. Save, print, and then close **2-PTMarqCost.xlsx**.

Performance Threads   **Assessment 2**   Completing and Formatting a Worksheet

Data Files

1. Open **PTMarqCostInv.xlsx** and save it with the name **2-PTMarqCostInv**.
2. Complete the invoice using the following information:

   a. Type the current date in cell G6.

   b. Refer to your electronic copy or printout of the costumes in Assessment 1. Type the values from the *Fee* column (the range K4:K10) into the appropriate cells in the range F15:F21.

   c. Create a formula to total the costume fees in cell F22. *Hint: Make sure the total agrees with the total costume fee on your printout from Assessment 1.*

   d. The transportation and storage container fee for each of the seven costumes is $75.00. Enter the appropriate formula in cell F24 that will calculate the fee for seven containers.

   e. Enter in cell F25 the delivery fee for all seven costumes: $250.00.

   f. Enter in cell F26 a formula that will add the total for the costume fees with the additional charges.

   g. Enter in cell F27 a formula that will calculate 13% Canadian Harmonized sales tax on the total in cell F26.

   h. Enter in cell F28 a formula to calculate the total invoice as the sum of cells F26 and F27.

3. Insert **PTLogo.jpg** in cell A1 and then resize it to fit in the three rows at the top left of the worksheet.

4. Improve the appearance of the worksheet by adjusting column widths, deleting blank rows, moving cells, and/or applying formatting features that you learned in this section.
5. Save, print, and then close **2-PTMarqCostInv.xlsx**.

Assessment 3 Performing a Spelling Check; Adjusting Column Width; Using Find and Replace; Inserting an Image; Applying Formatting Features

Data File

1. Open **WEMPRev.xlsx** and save it with the name **2-WEMPRev**.
2. Make the following corrections:
   a. Perform a spelling check.
   b. Adjust column widths so all data is completely visible.
   c. Change all of the venues named *Cinema House* to *Cinema Magic*.
   d. In cell A3, type Date: and then enter today's date in cell B3.
   e. Search for an image of a monarch butterfly and then insert the image at the top right of the worksheet.
   f. Improve the appearance of the worksheet by applying formatting features you learned in this section.
3. Save, print, and then close **2-WEMPRev.xlsx**.

Assessment 4 Finding Scaling Options

1. Open **WBInventory.xlsx** and then save it with the name **2-WBInventory**.
2. Use the Help feature to find out how to scale a worksheet so it fits on one page when printed.
3. Click the File tab and then click the *Print* option to display the Print backstage area.
4. Scale the worksheet so that it fits on one page at the Print backstage area.
5. Print, save, and then close **2-WBInventory.xlsx**.

INDIVIDUAL CHALLENGE **Assessment 5** Locating Information on Theatre Arts Programs

1. You are considering enrolling in a drama/theatre arts program at a college or university. Search the Internet for available programs in postsecondary schools in the United States and Canada. Choose three schools that interest you the most and find out as much as you can about the costs of attending these schools. Try to find information on costs beyond tuition and books, such as transportation and room and board.
2. Create a workbook that compares the costs for each of the three schools. For example, create the cost categories in column A and include three columns next to each cost category where you will enter the costs you found for each school. Total the costs for each of the schools.
3. Apply formatting features you learned in this section to the worksheet.
4. Save the workbook with the name **2-TheatreArts**.
5. Print and then close **2-TheatreArts.xlsx**.

Marquee Challenge

Challenge 1   Creating a Direct Wages Budget Report for a Film Shoot

1. You work with Chris Greenbaum, production manager at Marquee Productions. Chris has asked you to create the direct wages budget for the company's remote location film shoot. Create the worksheet shown in Figure WB-2.1. *Note: The logo is a file named MPLogo.jpg.*
2. Link the values in the *Estimated Daily Rates* table (columns I and J) to the *Daily Rate* column (column F) in the budget section.
3. Calculate the extended cost by summing the number of days for site prep, shoot, and cleanup and then multiplying by the daily rate.
4. Calculate the total in cell G16.
5. Apply formatting options as shown and then format the values in column G to an appropriate number format. Use your best judgment to determine the font, font size, column widths, borders, and fill colors.
6. Although not visible in the figure, a border should also be applied along the top (columns A–G) and left edges (rows 1–16) of the budget cells so that, when printed, the entire budget has a perimeter border.
7. Print the worksheet in landscape orientation and then save it with the name **2-MPLocBudg**.
8. Close **2-MPLocBudg.xlsx**.

Challenge 2   Creating a Room Timetable

1. You are an assistant to the person who schedules classroom space in the Theatre Arts Division at Niagara Peninsula College. You have been given the room schedule for the auditorium for next semester. The division posts a printed copy of the timetable outside the auditorium door so that students know when the room is available to work on projects and rehearse for upcoming plays. You want to use Excel to create and format the timetable so that the printed copy is easy to read and has a more professional appearance.
2. Refer to the data in Figure WB-2.2 and then create the timetable in a new workbook. Apply formatting features you learned in this section to create a colorful, easy-to-read room timetable.
3. Save the workbook with the name **2-NPCRoomSch**.
4. Print and then close **2-NPCRoomSch.xlsx**.

Figure WB-2.1 Challenge 1

	A	B	C	D	E	F	G	H	I	J
1										
2				MARQUEE						
3				PRODUCTIONS						
				Remove Location Film Shoot						
4				**July 11 to Agust 31, 2018**						
5				Direct Wages Budget						
6			Site Prep	Shoot	Cleanup	Daily	Extended		Estimated Daily Rates	
7	Personnel		Days	Days	Days	Rate	Cost		*Subject to Change*	
8	Crew		9	32	2				Crew	1,275
9	Cast		0	32	0				Cast	13,775
10	Actor Assistants		0	32	0				Actor Assistants	3,250
11	Extras		0	19	0				Extras	2,800
12	Cleaners		9	32	5				Cleaners	875
13	Security		7	32	5				Security	3,750
14	Administration		9	32	5				Administration	1,275
15										
16				Total Direct Wages Budget						
17										

Figure WB-2.2 Challenge 2

Niagara Peninsula College					
Room:	T1101		Period Covered: January 1 to April 30		
Time	Monday	Tuesday	Wednesday	Thursday	Friday
8:00 AM	SM100-01	AC215-03		MG210-01	SM240-03
9:00 AM	Prasad	McLean	LE100-03	Spelberger	Prasad
10:00 AM	LE253-03	(lab)	Das	SM355-02	SD350-04
11:00 AM	Das			Prasad	Attea
12:00 PM	SD451-01	PD250-02	Common	PD320-03	
1:00 PM	Attea	Kemper	Period	Kemper	LE310-02
2:00 PM	PD340-02	MG410-03	AC478-01	AC480-01	Das
3:00 PM	Kemper	Spelberger	Simmons	Simmons	MG210-01
4:00 PM	MG150-02	SM165-01	AC140-01	(lab)	Spelberger
5:00 PM	Spelberger	Prasad	Chou		

Use of this facility is restricted to staff and registered students only of Niagara Peninsula College. Failure to abide by this policy is considered a serious violation of the college's code of conduct.

Note 1:	Monday through Thursday evenings, room is booked for Continuing Education department.
Note 2:	Room is booked 8:00 AM to 5:00 PM the second Saturday of each month for the local community theatre group.

Study Tools

Study tools include a presentation and In Brief step lists. Use these resources to help you further develop and review skills learned in this section.

Knowledge Check

 SNAP Check your understanding by identifying application tools used in this section. If you are a SNAP user, launch the Knowledge Check from your Assignments page.

Recheck

 SNAP Check your understanding by taking this quiz. If you are a SNAP user, launch the Recheck from your Assignments page.

Skills Exercise

 SNAP Additional activities are available to SNAP users. If you are a SNAP user, access these activities from your Assignments page.

Skills Review

Review 1 **Inserting Statistical, Date, and IF Functions; Creating Range Names; Changing Page Layout Options**

Data File

1. Open **WBQtrRev.xlsx** and then save it with the name **3-WBQtrRev**.
2. Select the range B10:E10 and name it *TotalQtr*.
3. Make cell B12 active and then insert a formula that finds the average of the TotalQtr range.
4. Make cell B13 active and then insert a formula that finds the maximum total quarterly revenue in the TotalQtr range.
5. Make cell B14 active and then insert a formula that finds the minimum total quarterly revenue in the TotalQtr range.
6. Make cell B16 active and then name the cell *MinTarget*.
7. Make cell B17 active and then calculate how much under the minimum target the quarter's total revenue is if the minimum target was not met by typing the IF formula =if(b10<mintarget,b10-mintarget,0).
8. Copy the IF formula in cell B17 to the range C17:E17.
9. Make cell B19 active and then format the date in the cell to display as *#/##/##*.

10. Make cell B20 active and then insert a formula that adds 350 days to the date in cell B19.

11. Change to landscape orientation.

12. Change the top margin to 1.5 inches and center the worksheet horizontally.

13. Display the worksheet in Page Layout view and then create a header that prints your first and last names at the left margin and the current date at the right margin.

14. Create a footer that prints the file name at the bottom center of the page.

15. Save and then print **3-WBQtrRev.xlsx**.

Review 2 Creating Charts; Drawing Shapes

1. With **3-WBQtrRev.xlsx** open, select the range A3:E8 and then create a column chart by completing the following steps:

   a. Click the *Clustered Column* option in the *2-D Column* section.

   b. Move the chart to a new sheet and label the sheet *ColumnChart*.

   c. Apply the Layout 5 quick layout.

   d. Apply the Style 6 chart style.

   e. Change the chart title to *Quarterly Revenue Budget Forecast*.

   f. Select and then delete the Axis Title box that displays rotated at the left side of the chart.

2. Print the ColumnChart sheet.

3. Make Sheet1 the active sheet, select the ranges A3:A8 and F3:F8, and then create a pie chart by completing the following steps:

   a. Click the *Pie* option in the *2-D Pie* section.

   b. Move the chart to a new sheet and label the sheet *PieChart*.

   c. Apply the Layout 6 quick layout.

   d. Apply the Style 3 chart style.

   e. Change the chart title to *Total Revenue Budget Forecast*.

   f. Select the legend and then change the font size to 11 points.

4. With PieChart the active sheet, draw an Up Arrow Callout shape (last shape in second row in the *Block Arrows* group) in the pie chart by completing the following steps:

   a. Click the *Up Arrow Callout* shape and then click directly below the *55%* in the Dining room pie slice.

   b. Change the height of the shape to 1.4 inches and the width to 1.6 inches.

   c. Type This is a 10% increase over last year! inside the shape.

   d. Position the arrow below *55%* with the tip of the arrow touching the middle of the bottom border of the *55%*.

   e. With the shape selected, click the Home tab, click the Bold button in the Font group, and then click the Center button and the Middle Align button in the Alignment group.

5. Print the PieChart sheet.

6. Save and then close **3-WBQtrRev.xlsx**.

Skills Assessment

Note: If you submit your work in hard copy, check with your instructor before completing these Assessments to find out if you need to print two copies of each worksheet with one of the copies showing the cell formulas instead of the calculated results.

Assessment 1   Creating Statistical and IF Functions; Using Absolute References

1. Open **FCTSalesComm.xlsx** and then save it with the name **3-FCTSalesComm**.
2. Make cell D4 active and then write an IF statement using the information in the Commission table in the range F2:G4. Write the IF statement so that if the number of cruises booked is greater than 2, then Excel will multiply the total value of travel bookings by the commission percentage in cell G4, and if the condition is not met, Excel will insert a zero. Note: When a zero has the Accounting format applied, it displays as a hyphen instead of a 0. You will be copying the formula, so make sure cell G4 in the formula is an absolute reference.
3. Copy the IF function in cell D4 into cell D16.
4. Format the values in column D to match the formatting of the numbers in column B.
5. Type the label Average commission in cell B20 and create a function in cell D20 to calculate the average commission paid.
6. Type the label Maximum commission in cell B21 and create a function in cell D21 to show the highest commission paid.
7. Scale the worksheet to fit on one page.
8. Change the top margin to 1.25 inches and the left margin to 1.5 inches.
9. Save, print, and then close **3-FCTSalesComm.xlsx**.

Assessment 2   Applying the PMT Function

1. Open **WELoan.xlsx** and then save it with the name **3-WELoan**.
2. Calculate the monthly payments on the loan in cells B7 and D7.
3. Calculate the total payments required for each loan in cells B11 and D11.
4. Save, print, and then close **3-WELoan.xlsx**.

Assessment 3   Creating Charts; Drawing Shapes

1. Open **NPCGrades.xlsx** and then save it with the name **3-NPCGrades**.
2. Create a line chart in a new sheet labeled *LineChart* that displays the number of A+ through F grades earned for all five courses. Include an appropriate chart title. You determine the line chart style, layout, and any other chart elements and formats that will make the chart easy to interpret.
3. Create a 3-D pie chart that displays the total of each grade as a percentage of 100. ***Hint: Select the ranges B3:G3 and B9:G9 to create the chart***. Include an appropriate chart title and display percents around the outside of the pie slices as well as the category names. Position the pie chart below the grades worksheet, starting in row 11.

4. In the white space at the top left of the chart, draw a right-pointing block arrow pointing to the percent value above the pie slice for the F grade. Inside the block arrow type the text Lowest failure rate since 2014! If necessary, format the text to a smaller font to fit within the available space.
5. Print the worksheet centered horizontally and then print the line chart.
6. Save and then close **3-NPCGrades.xlsx**.

Assessment 4 Creating Charts; Changing Page Layout; Inserting a Footer

1. Open **FCTEurope.xlsx** and then save it with the name **3-FCTEurope**.
2. Create a 3-D Clustered Bar bar chart in a new sheet labeled *14NightsChart* that graphs the standard and deluxe rates for all of the destinations for 14 nights. Add an appropriate title to the chart and make any other formatting choices you think would enhance the chart.
3. Print the 14NightsChart sheet.
4. Create a 3-D Clustered Bar bar chart in a new sheet labeled *21NightsChart* that graphs the standard and deluxe rates for all of the destinations for 21 nights. Add an appropriate title to the chart and make any other formatting choices you think would enhance the chart.
5. Print the 21NightsChart sheet.
6. Make Sheet1 the active sheet, change to landscape orientation, change the top margin to 1.5 inches, and center the worksheet horizontally.
7. Create a custom footer that prints your name at the left margin and the file name at the right margin.
8. Print Sheet1.
9. Save and then close **3-FCTEurope.xlsx**.

Assessment 5 Finding Information on Chart Axis Options

1. Use the Help feature to find information on changing the vertical axis scale options in a chart. Use *change axis labels* as the search text.
2. Open **3-FCTEurope.xlsx**.
3. Make the 14NightsChart sheet active.
4. Using the information you learned in Help, change the value axis options so that the minimum bounds value is fixed at 1,000 and the major unit is fixed at 500. This means the value axis will start at $1,000 instead of zero and gridlines will show at every $500 interval. ***Hint: Make these changes in the Format Axis task pane with the Axis Options icon selected.***
5. Print the 14NightsChart sheet.
6. Save and then close **3-FCTEurope.xlsx**.

Assessment 6   Social Networking Survey

1. You want to know which social networking tool and which social activity is the most popular among your friends, family, and classmates. Ask 10 to 20 friends, family, or classmates the following two questions and collect the responses in an Excel worksheet.
   a. Which of the following social networking sites do you use?

Facebook	Instagram
Pinterest	Twitter

   b. Which social networking activities do you do at these sites?

Share photos	Share family updates
Promote a blog	Share media
Meet people	

2. Create a chart in a new sheet labeled *SocialNetSites* that displays the total users for each of the social networking sites in the first survey question. You determine the most appropriate chart type to display the survey results. Add an appropriate chart title and any other chart formatting options to enhance the chart's appearance.

3. Print the SocialNetSites sheet.

4. Create a chart in a new sheet labeled *SocialNetAct* that displays the total participants for each type of social networking activity in the second survey question. You determine the appropriate chart type to display the survey results. Add an appropriate chart title and any other chart formatting options to enhance the chart's appearance.

5. Print the SocialNetAct sheet.

6. Save the workbook and name it **3-SocialNetSurvey**.

7. Print the worksheet with the source data for the two charts and then close **3-SocialNetSurvey.xlsx**.

Marquee Challenge

Challenge 1   Creating Charts on Movie Attendance Statistics

1. You are working with Shannon Grey, president of Marquee Productions, on presentation materials for an upcoming staff development workshop on producing and marketing movies. As part of Shannon's research for the workshop, she compiled a workbook with statistics related to movie attendance by age group and by household income. Shannon has asked you to create two charts for the workshop based on this source data. To begin, open **MPMovieStats.xlsx** and then save it with the name **3-MPMovieStats**.

2. Using data in the workbook, create the bar chart in Figure WB-3.1 with the following specifications:
   a. Create a 3-D Clustered Bar chart.
   b. Move the chart to a new sheet and name the sheet *AgeChart*.
   c. Apply the Style 6 chart style.
   d. Change the font for the title to 20-point Cambria bold.
   e. Add the primary horizontal axis to the chart using the Chart Elements button. *Hint: Expand the* **Axes** *option and then insert a check mark in the* **Primary Horizontal** *check box.*

f. Change the font for the axes (information at the left and bottom) to 12-point Cambria bold and change the font color to White, Background 1.

g. Insert the shape with the Down Arrow Callout shape in the *Block Arrows* section.

h. Make any other formatting changes so your chart looks like the chart in Figure WB-3.1.

3. Using data in the workbook, create the Doughnut chart in Figure WB-3.2 with the following specifications:

a. Create a Doughnut chart. (Use the Insert Pie or Doughnut Chart button in the Charts group on the Insert tab to find the doughnut chart.)

b. Move the chart to a new sheet and name the sheet *IncomeChart*.

c. Apply the Style 3 chart style.

d. Apply the Layout 5 chart layout.

e. Change the font for the title to 20-point Cambria bold.

f. Insert the 8-Point Star shape (fifth column, first row in the *Stars and Banners* section).

g. Make any other formatting changes so your chart looks like the chart in Figure WB-3.2.

4. Save the revised workbook.

5. Print each chart and then close **3-MPMovieStats.xlsx**.

Figure WB-3.1 Challenge 1 Bar Chart

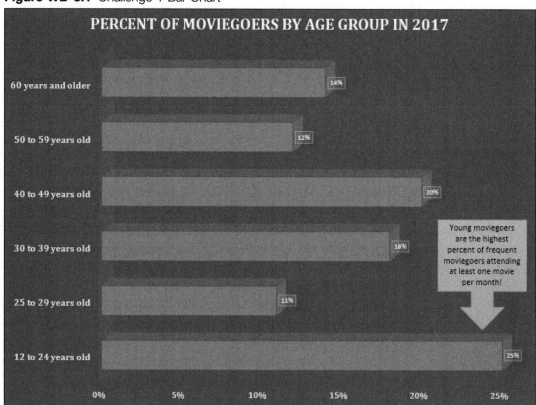

Figure WB-3.2 Challenge 1 Doughnut Chart

Challenge 2   Preparing an International Student Report

1. You work in the Registrar's Office at Niagara Peninsula College. Terri VanDaele, the registrar, has sent you a workbook with the top 10 countries of origin for international students registered for the 2018 academic year. Terri would like you to format the workbook to improve the appearance and create a chart next to the data for inclusion with the annual report to the board. To begin, open **NPCTop10Int.xlsx** and then save it with the name **3-NPCTop10Int**.
2. Using the data in the workbook, create the chart shown in Figure WB-3.3. Create a 2-D clustered column chart, apply the Style 4 chart style, and delete the title. Size and move the chart so it is positioned as shown in the figure.
3. Insert and position the Niagara Peninsula College logo as shown in the figure using the **NPCLogo.jpg** file.
4. Insert the image **GlobeHands.jpg** and then size and move the image so it appears as shown in the figure.
5. Make sure the workbook fits on one page. If it does not, change to landscape orientation.
6. Save, print, and then close **3-NPCTop10Int.xlsx**.

Figure WB-3.3 Challenge 2

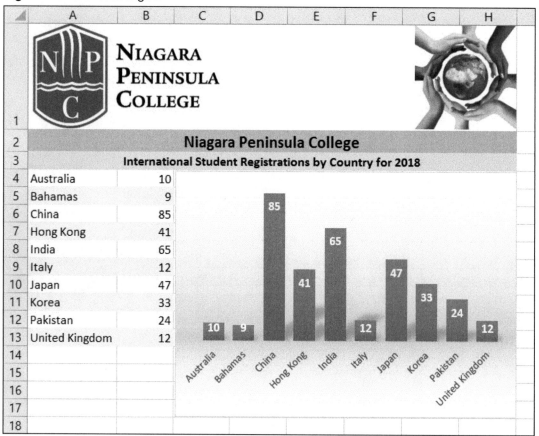

Microsoft®

Access®

Study Tools

Study tools include a presentation and In Brief step lists. Use these resources to help you further develop and review skills learned in this section.

Knowledge Check

SNAP Check your understanding by identifying application tools used in this section. If you are a SNAP user, launch the Knowledge Check from your Assignments page.

Recheck

SNAP Check your understanding by taking this quiz. If you are a SNAP user, launch the Recheck from your Assignments page.

Skills Exercise

SNAP Additional activities are available to SNAP users. If you are a SNAP user, access these activities from your Assignments page.

Skills Review

Review 1   **Adjusting Column Widths; Finding and Editing Records; Adding and Deleting Records**

Data File

1. Open **1-WEEmployees.accdb** and enable the contents, if necessary.
2. Open the Employees table.
3. Adjust all column widths to accommodate the longest entries.
4. Find the record for Carl Zakowski and then change the birth date from *5/9/1967* to *12/22/1987*.
5. Find the record for Roman Deptulski and then change the salary from *$69,725.00* to *$72,750.00*. ***Note: You do not need to type the dollar symbol, comma, decimal, or digits after the decimal point***.
6. Find the record for Terry Yiu and then change the hire date from *4/12/2012* to *1/31/2018*.
7. Delete the record for Valerie Fitsouris.
8. Delete the record for Edward Thurston.

9. Add the following records to the table in the appropriate fields.
   Note: In this table, **EmployeeID** *is not an AutoNumber data type field; therefore, you will need to type the numbers in the first field.*

1085	1090	1095
Yousef J Armine	Maria D Quinte	Patrick J Kilarney
11/19/1992	4/16/1993	2/27/1987
3/14/2018	11/29/2018	12/12/2018
European Distribution	Overseas Distribution	North American Distribution
$42,177	$42,177	$42,177

10. Close the Employees table. Click Yes when prompted to save changes.

Worldwide Enterprises

Review 2 Sorting; Previewing; Changing Margins and Page Orientation; Filtering; Hiding Columns; Printing

1. With **1-WEEmployees.accdb** open, open the Employees table.
2. Sort the table in ascending order by *LastName*.
3. Preview the table in the Print Preview window.
4. Change to landscape orientation.
5. Change the top margin to 1.5 inches and the left margin to 1.25 inches using options at the Page Setup dialog box with the Print Options tab selected.
6. Print the table.
7. Filter the table to display only those employees who work in the European Distribution Department.
8. Hide the *EmployeeID* field column.
9. Print the table and then close the Employees table. Click Yes when prompted to save changes.
10. Close **1-WEEmployees.accdb**.

Skills Assessment

NIAGARA PENINSULA COLLEGE

Data File

Assessment 1 Adjusting Column Width; Finding and Editing Records; Previewing and Printing

1. Open **1-NPCGrades.accdb** and enable the contents, if necessary.
2. Open the SM100-01Grades table.
3. Adjust all column widths to accommodate the longest entries.
4. Enter the following grades in the appropriate records:

Terry Yiu	A+	Kevin Gibson	C
Maren Bastow	C	Ash Bhullar	A
Martine Gagne	B	Bruce Morgan	B
Armado Ennis	D	Russell Clements	A
Bentley Woollatt	B	Richard Loewen	F
Susan Retieffe	C		

5. Preview and then print the table.
6. Close the SM100-01Grades table. Click Yes when prompted to save changes.
7. Close **1-NPCGrades.accdb**.

Data File

Assessment 2   Finding, Adding, and Deleting Records; Formatting Datasheet

1. Open **1-WBInventory.accdb** and enable the contents, if necessary.
2. Open the InventoryList table.
3. Adjust all column widths to accommodate the longest entry.
4. Locate and then delete the records for the inventory items *Pita Wraps*, *Tuna*, and *Lake Erie Perch*.
5. Add the following new records to the InventoryList table.

ItemNo	ItemDescription	Unit	SupplierCode
051	Atlantic Scallops	case	9
052	Lake Trout	case	9
053	Panini Rolls	flat	1

6. Change the font size for all data in the table to 10 points.
7. Preview the table in Print Preview and, if necessary, adjust the top and/or bottom margin settings until all of the records will print on one page and then print the table.
8. Close the InventoryList table. Click Yes when prompted to save changes.
9. Close **1-WBInventory.accdb**.

Data File

Assessment 3   Finding, Sorting, Filtering, and Deleting Records

1. Open **1-PTCostumeInv.accdb** and enable the contents, if necessary.
2. Open the CostumeInventory table.
3. Adjust all column widths to accommodate the longest entry.
4. Locate and then delete the records for the following costumes that were destroyed in a fire at a Shakespearean festival:

Macbeth	Othello
Lady Macbeth	King Lear
Hamlet	Richard III

5. Sort the table in ascending order by the *CostumeTitle* field.
6. Preview the table, adjust the margins so that all data fits on one page, and then print the table.
7. Filter the table so that only those records that were rented out on 10/1/2018 are displayed.
8. Print the filtered list.
9. Redisplay all records.
10. Clear the filter from the table.
11. Close the CostumeInventory table. Click Yes when prompted to save changes.
12. Close **1-PTCostumeInv.accdb**.

NIAGARA PENINSULA COLLEGE

Assessment 4   Using the Filter by Form Feature

1. Using the Access Help window, locate and then open the article *Filter data in a desktop database*. Scroll down the article and locate the information on different ways to filter. Learn specifically how to use the Filter by Form feature.
2. Open **1-NPCGrades.accdb** and enable the contents, if necessary.
3. Open the AC215-03Grades table.

4. Using the Filter by Form feature, filter those records with a grade of *A+* or *F*.
5. Print the filtered table.
6. Clear the filter from the table.
7. Close the table without saving changes and then close the database.
8. Open Microsoft Word and then use one of the memo templates to create a memo addressed to your instructor that lists the steps you completed to filter the grades using the Filter by Form feature.
9. Save the memo and name it **1-FilterMemo**.
10. Print and then close **1-FilterMemo.docx**.
11. Close Word.

Assessment 5   Creating a Job Search Company Database

1. You are starting to plan ahead for your job search after graduation. You decide to maintain a database of company information in Access. To begin, search the Internet for at least eight companies in your field of study (four out of state or out of province). Include company name, address, and telephone number, and a contact person in the Human Resources Department, if possible.
2. Open **1-JobSearchInfo.accdb** and enable the contents, if necessary.
3. Open the CompanyInfo table. (The table contains eight records; you will be adding at least eight additional records.)
4. Enter at least eight additional records for the companies you researched on the Internet.
5. Adjust column widths as necessary.
6. Sort the records in ascending order by the *CompanyName* field.
7. Preview the table and make any changes required to ensure that the table prints on one page.
8. Print and then close the CompanyInfo table.
9. Close **1-JobSearchInfo.accdb**.

Marquee Challenge

Challenge 1   Updating and Printing a Catering Events Table

1. Open **1-WBSpecialEvents.accdb** and enable the contents, if necessary.
2. Open the CateringContracts table.
3. Dana Hirsch, manager, has given you information related to five new catering events that were recently booked at the bistro. Dana would like you to add to the table the information shown in Figure WB-1.1. Dana advises that deposits have been received for all of these events. The columns in the table that have check boxes displayed are defined as Yes/No fields. In these columns, click to insert a check mark in the box indicating "Yes"; otherwise leave the check box empty to indicate "No."
4. Jack Torrance has called and canceled his business meeting on May 15. Delete the record.

5. Dana would like the charge for the Pavelich wedding updated to $33.50 per person.
6. Dana would like a printout of the table with the records sorted by customers' last names and the *ID* and *ContactPhone* fields hidden.
7. Make sure the data is entirely visible in all columns and that the printout is only one page, and then print the table.
8. Close the CateringContracts table, saving design changes.
9. Close **1-WBSpecialEvents.accdb**.

Figure WB-1.1 Challenge 1

Name	Phone	Event	Date	Room	Guests	Charge	Special Menu
Cora Spriet	905 555 1623	Wedding	8/4/2018	Westview	150	26.95	Yes
Sean Vezina	716 555 3846	Business Meeting	8/13/2018	Starlake	24	23.75	No
William Graham	716 555 8694	25th Wedding Anniversary	8/18/2018	Sunset	80	24.95	No
Helen Kosjovic	716 555 3441	Engagement Brunch	8/19/2018	Sunset	56	22.95	No
Pieter Borman	716 555 6994	Business Meeting	8/22/2018	Starlake	41	24.95	Yes

 **Challenge 2   Determining Fields and Table Names for a New Database**

1. Bobbie Sinclair, business manager, is considering having you create a new database to store the custom costume business at Performance Threads. Bobbie has jotted down rough notes regarding the information to be stored in the new database in Figure WB-1.2. Using Microsoft Word, create a document that provides the proposed field names and table names for each table. Incorporate the information in the additional notes as you develop the tables. As you create this document, consider the following two database design practices:
   • The use of spaces in field names or table names is discouraged.
   • Within each table, one field must contain unique identifying information.
2. At this stage of the design process, you are only considering the breakdown of fields to accommodate the information in Figure WB-1.2. Do not be concerned with other elements of the table and database design, such as data type, properties, and relationships.
3. Save the Word document and name it **1-PTCostumes**.
4. Print and then close the document.

Figure WB-1.2 Challenge 2

Customer Information Customer's name, address, contact telephone numbers	Order Information Description of costume Customer for whom costume is being made Contract price Date due Seamstress Estimated hours for each of the main cost centers: Research, Design, Production Deposit amount received in advance
Contract Seamstresses Name, address, and contact telephone numbers for seamstresses on contract with Performance Threads	Ship To Information Customer Costume Address for delivery of costume Shipping company Shipping charge

Additional notes:
- Costumes are quoted a contract price, which the customer accepts in advance by signing a contract document. The signed document must be on file before work begins.
- The hours for the three cost centers are estimated at the time of the quote. Robbie wants to use the database to also enter actual hours after the costume is complete to generate hours-variance reports.

Study Tools

Study tools include a presentation and In Brief step lists. Use these resources to help you further develop and review skills learned in this section.

Knowledge Check

SNAP Check your understanding by identifying application tools used in this section. If you are a SNAP user, launch the Knowledge Check from your Assignments page.

Recheck

SNAP Check your understanding by taking this quiz. If you are a SNAP user, launch the Recheck from your Assignments page.

Skills Exercise

SNAP Additional activities are available to SNAP users. If you are a SNAP user, access these activities from your Assignments page.

Skills Review

Review 1 Creating and Modifying a Table in Design View

1. Open **2-WEEmployeeData.accdb** and enable the contents, if necessary.
2. Create a table in Design view using the following field names and data types. You decide whether to add an appropriate description. Do *not* set any field properties since these will be changed later in this activity.

Field Name	Data Type
EmployeeID	Short Text
SupervisorLName	Short Text
SupervisorFName	Short Text
AnnualRevDate	Date/Time
SalaryIncDate	Date/Time
ProfDevDays	Number

3. Set the *EmployeeID* field as the primary key field.
4. Save the table and name it *Review*.

5. Switch to Datasheet view and then enter the following two records:

EmployeeID	1013	EmployeeID	1030
SupervisorLName	Vestering	SupervisorLName	Deptulski
SupervisorFName	Sam	SupervisorFName	Roman
AnnualRevDate	2/10/18	AnnualRevDate	1/22/19
SalaryIncDate	9/01/18	SalaryIncDate	7/22/19
ProfDevDays	5	ProfDevDays	10

6. Adjust all columns to best fit the longest entries.
7. Save the changes to the table layout.
8. Switch to Design view and then make the following changes to the field properties:
   a. Change the field size for the *EmployeeID* field to 4 characters.
   b. Create a validation rule for the *ProfDevDays* field to ensure that no number greater than 10 is entered into the field. Enter an appropriate validation text error message.
   c. Save the table and click Yes at the message that indicates some data may be lost and to test the data with the new validation rule.
   d. Create an input mask for both date fields to set the pattern for entering dates to the Medium Date format. Use the default entry for the placeholder character. Click Yes if prompted to save the table before displaying the Input Mask Wizard.
   e. Change the setting in the *Format* property box so both date fields display the date in the Medium Date format.
9. Save the table.
10. Switch to Datasheet view and add the following two records:

EmployeeID	1040	EmployeeID	1043
SupervisorLName	Ruiz	SupervisorLName	Deptulski
SupervisorFName	Celesta	SupervisorFName	Roman
AnnualRevDate	10-Mar-19	AnnualRevDate	15-Aug-18
SalaryIncDate	01-Sep-19	SalaryIncDate	01-Feb-19
ProfDevDays	8	ProfDevDays	6

11. Display the table in Print Preview.
12. Change to landscape orientation and then print the table.
13. Close Print Preview and then close the Review table.

Worldwide Enterprises

Review 2   Modifying, Moving, and Deleting Fields; Creating Relationships

1. With **2-WEEmployeeData.accdb** open, open the Review table in Design view.
2. Move the *ProfDevDays* field between *SupervisorFName* and *AnnualRevDate*.
3. Move *SupervisorFName* before *SupervisorLName*.
4. Add caption properties so the fields display the following headings in Datasheet view:

   Supervisor First Name   Annual Review Date
   Supervisor Last Name   Salary Increase Date
   Professional Development Days

5. Save the table, switch to Datasheet view, adjust all column widths as necessary, and then print the datasheet in landscape orientation and with the left and right margins set to 0.5 inch.

6. Close the Review table, saving changes to the layout.
7. Open the Employees table in Design view.
8. Delete the *Supervisor* field.
9. Save and then close the Employees table.
10. Open the Relationships window.
11. Click the Show Table button in the Relationships group on the Relationship Tools Design tab, add the Review table to the window, and then close the Show Table dialog box.
12. Create a one-to-one relationship between the Employees table (primary table) and the Review table (related table) using the *EmployeeID* field. Turn on referential integrity.
13. Save the changes to the relationships.
14. Generate a new relationship report and then print the report in landscape orientation.
15. Save the new report, naming it *Relationships*, and then close the report.
16. Close the Relationships window and then close **2-WEEmployeeData.accdb**.

Skills Assessment

Data File

Assessment 1   Creating a Table in Design View; Creating a Lookup Field

1. Open **2-NPCGrades.accdb** and enable the contents, if necessary.
2. Create a new table in Design view using the following field names: *StudentNo*; *LastName*; *FirstName*; *Grade*. Set the data type to *Short Text* for each field except *Grade*. At the *Grade* field, use the Lookup Wizard to create a drop-down list with the following grades: *A+, A, B, C, D, F*.
3. Restrict the *Grade* lookup properties to items within the list only and do not allow the values within the list to be edited from the datasheet.
4. Set the *StudentNo* field as the primary key field.
5. Save the table and name it AC478-01Grades.
6. Enter the following four records in the table in Datasheet view:

StudentNo	111-785-156	*StudentNo*	118-487-578
LastName	Bastow	*LastName*	Andre
FirstName	Maren	*FirstName*	Ian
Grade	A+	*Grade*	C
StudentNo	137-845-746	*StudentNo*	138-456-749
LastName	Knowlton	*LastName*	Yiu
FirstName	Sherri	*FirstName*	Terry
Grade	B	*Grade*	D

7. Adjust all column widths to best fit the longest entries.
8. Print and then close the AC478-01Grades table, saving changes.
9. Close **2-NPCGrades.accdb**.

1. Open **2-PTCostumeInv.accdb** and enable the contents, if necessary.
2. Open the CostumeInventory table in Design view.
3. Change the *DateIn* field to a Date/Time data type field.
4. Change the field size for *CostumeNo* to 5 characters to limit the field to the number of characters Performance Threads assigns to a costume inventory item.
5. Performance Threads has a minimum daily rental fee of $85.00. Create a validation rule and validation text entry that will ensure no one enters a value less than $85.00 in the *DailyRentalFee* field.
6. To ensure no one switches the order of the month and day when entering the *DateOut* and *DateIn* fields, create an input mask for these two fields to require that the date be entered in the Medium Date format.
7. Since Performance Threads is open seven days a week, format the *DateOut* and *DateIn* fields to display the dates in the Long Date format. This adds the day of the week to the entry and spells the month in full.
8. Save the table and then switch to Datasheet view.
9. Change the font size of the data in the table to 10 points and then adjust all column widths to best fit the longest entries. (Access displays pound symbols (#) across a column when the width is not wide enough to display the data.)
10. Preview the table. Change the margins for the page as necessary so that the entire table fits on one page.
11. Save, print, and then close the CostumeInventory table.
12. Close **2-PTCostumeInv.accdb**.

Assessment 3   Creating a New Database

1. Create a new database on your storage medium named **2-FCTExpenses**.
2. Look at the sample expense form in Figure WB-2.1. Make a list of the fields that would be needed to store the information from this form in a table. You do not need to include fields for the mailing address for the employee. For each field in your list, determine the appropriate data type and field properties that could be used.
3. Create a new table so that Access creates an *ID* field automatically that you can use as the primary key field. Use the design information you created in Step 2 to enter the field names, data types, and field properties in the table.
4. Switch to Datasheet view and then enter the expense claim information shown in Figure WB-2.1 in a record.
5. Make sure all column headings and data are entirely visible.
6. Display the table in Print Preview, make any necessary changes to ensure that the table will print on one page, and then print the table.
7. Close **2-FCTExpenses.accdb**.

Figure WB-2.1 Assessment 3

Expense Statement

Employee Information

Name:	Terry Blessing	Emp ID:	LA-104
Address:	3341 Ventura Boulevard	Position:	President
City, State, ZIP:	Los Angeles, CA 90102	Manager:	Not required

Expense Claim Details

Date	Description	TOTAL CLAIMED
3/26/2018	Travel expenses to Toronto office for meeting	$2,344.10

NOTE: All expense claims must have original receipts attached.

Signature_____

Assessment 4   Finding Information on Templates

1. Use the Help feature to find information on how to find and download a template and then read the article titled *Where do I find templates?* If this article is not available, determine how to search for templates at the New backstage area.
2. Search for a contact template. When contact templates display in the New backstage area, double-click one of the templates such as a personal contact manager template or a contacts template. (If a welcome window displays, click the Close button in the upper right corner of the window.) Enable the contents of the downloaded file.
3. If necessary, expand the Navigation pane by clicking the Shutter Bar Open/Close Button.
4. Open one of the tables in the database and then enter at least one record in the table. (You determine the data.)
5. Adjust all column widths to best fit the longest entries.
6. Print the table containing the record you entered.
7. Save the database with the name **2-Contacts**.
8. Close **2-Contacts.accdb**.

INDIVIDUAL CHALLENGE

Assessment 5   Investigating Employment/Job Websites

1. Using the Internet, search for popular employment and/or job websites.
2. Create a new database on your storage medium named **2-JobWebsites**.
3. Create a table named *Websites* using Design view. Include fields to store the employment/job website name and the site's URL and then add a Long Text data type field in which you can type a brief note about the site's purpose. Include an *ID* field as the primary key field.

4. Save the table and then add at least three records to the datasheet for the sites you investigated in Step 1.
5. Preview and then print the Websites table, adjusting page layout options as necessary to minimize paper use.
6. Save and close the Websites table.
7. Close **2-JobWebsites**.

Marquee Challenge

Challenge 1 Modifying Tables and Creating a Table

1. Open **2-FCTTours.accdb** and enable the contents, if necessary.
2. Open the Tours table in Design view and then make the following changes:
   a. Move the *Tour* field between the *TourID* and *BegDate* fields.
   b. Delete the *Discount* field.
   c. Change the field size of the *TourID* field to 4 characters.
   d. This table contains tours only for the year 2019. Include a validation rule for the *BegDate* field that limits entries to dates after (greater than) 12/31/2018. Include appropriate validation text that will display if an incorrect date is entered in the field. Include a validation rule for the *EndDate* field that limits entries to dates before (less than) 1/1/2020. Include appropriate validation text that will display if an incorrect date is entered in the field.
   e. Enter the following records in the table. (Try entering incorrect dates in the *BegDate* and *EndDate* fields to determine if your validation rules work.)

TourID	HS04		TourID	BZ03
Tour	Hawaiian Special		Tour	Brazil Highlights
BegDate	4/3/2019		BegDate	4/24/2019
EndDate	4/9/2019		EndDate	5/4/2019
PriceSO	$1,899		PriceSO	$3,699
PriceDO	$1,659		PriceDO	$3,279

   f. Adjust column widths to best fit the longest enties.
   g. Save, print, and then close the Tours table.
3. Open the Agents table in Design view and then make the following changes:
   a. Delete the *HireDate* field.
   b. Change the field size of the *AgentID* field to 3 characters.
   c. Use the Lookup Wizard to specify the following choices for the *Office* field: *Los Angeles*, *San Francisco*, and *Toronto*.
   d. Enter the following records in the table:

AgentID	107		AgentID	131
FirstName	Jenna		FirstName	Rene
LastName	Williamson		LastName	Forbrege
OfficePhone	213-555-0939		OfficePhone	905-555-4321
CellPhone	562-555-3495		CellPhone	647-555-4389
Office	Los Angeles		Office	Toronto

4. Save, print, and then close the Agents table.

5. Create a new Bookings table with the fields shown below. You determine the field names and data types. Include appropriate captions for some or all of the fields. Change the field number size where appropriate and identify the *BookingID* field as the primary key field.

    BookingID (specify the AutoNumber data type and set as the primary key field)
    BookingDate (date the booking was made by the agent)
    TourID (the tour identification number from the Tours table)
    AgentID (the agent identification number from the Agents table)
    NumberPersons (number of people booked on a specific tour)

Include the following records in the table:

BookingID	(Access inserts number)	*BookingID*	(Access inserts number)
BookingDate	6/12/2018	*BookingDate*	6/14/2018
TourID	AF02	*TourID*	HC01
AgentID	114	*AgentID*	109
NumberPersons	8	*NumberPersons*	2
BookingID	(Access inserts number)	*BookingID*	(Access inserts number)
BookingDate	6/16/2018	*BookingDate*	6/16/2018
TourID	CR02	*TourID*	AK01
AgentID	103	*AgentID*	137
NumberPersons	2	*NumberPersons*	4
BookingID	(Access inserts number)	*BookingID*	(Access inserts number)
BookingDate	6/18/2018	*BookingDate*	6/19/2018
TourID	HC01	*TourID*	AT02
AgentID	109	*AgentID*	109
NumberPersons	2	*NumberPersons*	4

6. Save, print, and then close the Bookings table.
7. Create a one-to-many relationship that joins the Agents table with the Bookings table. (You determine the field that joins the two tables.) ***Hint: If you receive an error message when establishing a relationship, check to make sure that all the field types and field sizes are similar in the fields you are trying to join.***
8. Create a one-to-many relationship that joins the Tours table with the Bookings table. (You determine the field that joins the two tables.)
9. Create and print a relationship report and then close the Relationships window without saving the changes.
10. Close **2-FCTTours.accdb**.

Worldwide Enterprises

Data File

Challenge 2   Refining Tables in a Database; Creating Relationships

1. Open **2-WEPurchases.accdb** and enable the contents, if necessary.
2. Open each table and look at the sample data entered and then, in Design view, modify field properties to maximize Access features that can control or otherwise validate data entered. Consider the following practices at Worldwide Enterprises as you complete this task:
   a. Worldwide uses a 4-character purchase order numbering system.
   b. All vendors are assigned a 3-character vendor number.
   c. Staff at Worldwide are used to entering dates in the format dd-mmm-yy.

d. Telephone numbers must include the area code in parentheses, for example, (212) 555-6549.

e. Worldwide will not issue a purchase order for corporate wear that has a value less than $300.00.

3. Set up a new field in the Purchases table to enter the shipment method. Worldwide will only receive shipments from the following carriers with whom credit accounts have been set up: UPS, FedEx, Express Freight, and Global Transport. After creating the new field, populate the existing records with one of the carrier companies to test the field.

4. Create a relationship between the Vendors table and the Purchases table.

5. Create and print a relationship report.

6. Print each table, making sure all data is visible and minimizing paper use.

7. Using Microsoft Word, create a memo to your instructor that documents the field properties you modified in each table, including the property box entry you made. Save the memo and name it **2-Memo**. Print and then close the memo. Close Word.

8. Close **2-WEPurchases.accdb**.

Study Tools

Study tools include a presentation and In Brief step lists. Use these resources to help you further develop and review skills learned in this section.

Knowledge Check

SNAP Check your understanding by identifying application tools used in this section. If you are a SNAP user, launch the Knowledge Check from your Assignments page.

Recheck

SNAP Check your understanding by taking this quiz. If you are a SNAP user, launch the Recheck from your Assignments page.

Skills Exercise

 SNAP Additional activities are available to SNAP users. If you are a SNAP user, access these activities from your Assignments page.

Skills Review

 **Review 1** **Creating a Query Using the Simple Query Wizard; Sorting a Query; Performing Calculations; Extracting Records**

Data File

1. Open **3-WEEmployeeData.accdb** and enable the contents, if necessary.
2. Use the Simple Query Wizard to create a query that displays fields from the Employees and Benefits tables in order as follows:

Employees	Benefits
EmployeeID	*LifeInsce*
FirstName	
LastName	
HireDate	
AnnualSalary	

3. Accept the default Detail query and then type LifeInsceList as the title for the query.
4. View the query results datasheet and then switch to Design view.
5. Sort the query results by the *LastName* field in ascending order.
6. Insert a calculation in the field to the right of *LifeInsce* that divides *AnnualSalary* by 12. Label the new column *MonthlySalary*.
7. Format *MonthlySalary* to display the calculated values in the Currency format.
8. Save and run the query and then adjust the column width of *MonthlySalary* to best fit the entries.

9. Print the query results datasheet with the left and right margins at 0.5 inch.
10. Use Save Object As to copy the query design and name it *HiresAfter2015*.
11. If necessary, switch to Design view and then type >December 31, 2015 in the field in the *Criteria* row in the *HireDate* column. ***Note: Access will convert the text you type to >#12/31/2015# after you press the Enter key***.
12. Save and then run the query.
13. Print the query results datasheet with the left and right margins set to 0.5 inch and then close the HiresAfter2015 query.

Review 2   Creating and Modifying a Form

1. With **3-WEEmployeeData.accdb** open, create a new form for the Review table using the Form button.
2. With the form open in Layout view, make the following changes to the form design:
    a. Add the logo named **WELogo-Small.jpg** to the top left of the form and then resize the image until the entire logo is visible.
    b. Change the title text to *Annual Review and Salary Increase Dates*.
    c. Change the font size of the title text to 20 points.
    d. Resize the text box control objects containing the data to align at the right edge of the objects below the right side of the word *Salary* in the title text. (The Status bar should display *Lines: 1 Characters: 24*.)
3. Save the revised form, accepting the default name *Review*.
4. Switch to Form view and then display the Print dialog box. Click *Selected Record(s)* in the *Print Range* section of the Print dialog box and then click OK.
5. Close the form. Click Yes if prompted to save changes to the form's design.

Review 3   Creating and Modifying a Report

1. With **3-WEEmployeeData.accdb** open, use the Report button to create a report based on the LifeInsceList query you created in Review 1.
2. With the report open in Layout view, make the following changes to the report design:
    a. Add the logo named **WELogo-Small.jpg** to the top of the report and then resize the image as needed until the entire logo is visible.
    b. Change the title text to *Salary and Life Insurance Report*.
    c. Change the font size of the title text to 20 points.
    d. Change to landscape orientation.
    e. Move the *Life Insurance* column between the *HireDate* and *AnnualSalary* columns. ***Hint: Select from the control object containing the column heading, Life Insurance, through the total row at the bottom of the column before moving the column.***
    f. Decrease the width of the *FirstName* and *LastName* columns approximately one inch. (The Status bar should display *Lines: 1 Characters: 12*.)
    g. Edit column heading labels for those field names that do not have a space between compound words. For example, change *FirstName* to *First Name*.
3. Apply the Integral report theme.
4. Click in the date control object and then press the Delete key. Click in the time control object and then press the Delete key.

5. Scroll to the bottom of the report. Select and then delete any totals that appear below columns and then select and delete the page number. *Note: You may also have to delete an underscore line before a total. To do this, click the field where the line appears and then press the Delete key.*

6. Display the report in Print Preview. Click the Columns button in the Page Layout group on the Print Preview tab. Select the current measurement in the *Width* measurement box, type 8, and then press the Enter key.

7. Save the report, accepting the default name *LifeInsceList*.

8. Print and then close the report.

9. Close **3-WEEmployeeData.accdb**.

Skills Assessment

Assessment 1   Creating a Query in Design View; Sorting a Query; Extracting Records Using Multiple Criteria

1. Open **3-NPCGrades.accdb** and enable the contents, if necessary.

2. Create a query in Design view that extracts the records of those students with an A+ grade in all three courses using the following specifications:

   a. Add all three tables to the query design grid and then drag the primary key field name from the first table field list box to the second table field list box. This creates a join line between the first two tables on the *StudentNo* field.

   b. Drag the primary key field from the second table field list box to the third table field list box to create a join line between the second and third tables on the *StudentNo* field.

   c. Include in the query results the student number, first name, last name, and grade from the first table field list box and sort in ascending order by last name.

   d. Add the grade field from the second and third tables to the query design grid.

   e. Enter the required criteria statements to select the records of those students who achieved A+ in all three courses. *Hint: Type A+ encased in quotation marks ("A+") in the* **Criteria** *row to indicate the plus symbol is not part of a mathematical expression.*

3. Save the query and name it *A+Students*.

4. Run the query.

5. Adjust the columns to best fit the entries in the query results datasheet.

6. Print the query results datasheet in landscape orientation.

7. Close the A+Students query, saving changes, and then close **3-NPCGrades.accdb**.

Assessment 2   Creating a Query and Report; Modifying a Report

1. Open **3-PTCostumeInv.accdb** and enable the contents, if necessary.

2. Create a new query in Design view using the CostumeInventory table that lists fields in the following order: *CostumeNo, DateOut, DateIn, CostumeTitle, DailyRentalFee*.

3. Type the following criterion statement in the *DateOut* column to extract records for costumes rented in the months of July and August 2018:

   Between July 1, 2018 and August 31, 2018

4. Expand the column width of the *DateOut* column to view the entire criterion statement. Access converted the long dates to short dates and added pound symbols to the beginning and end of dates in the criterion statement.

5. Sort the query results in ascending order first by the *DateOut* field.
6. Save the query and name it *Summer2018Rentals*.
7. Run the query.
8. Print and then close the query.
9. Create a report based on the Summer2018Rentals query using the Report button.
10. Add the logo image **PTLogo-Small.jpg** to the top of the report and then resize the image as needed so that the entire logo is visible.
11. Change the title text to *Costume Rentals for July and August 2018* and then change the font size to 20 points.
12. Delete the control objects containing the current date and current time.
13. Delete the total amount and underscore line at the bottom of the *DailyRentalFee* field column.
14. Adjust column widths in the report until all columns fit on the page in portrait orientation. Move and/or resize any other control objects as necessary so that the entire report fits on one page to print. ***Hint: Make sure you check the page numbering control objects at the bottom of the page***.
15. Save the report, accepting the default name *Summer2018Rentals*, and then print the report.
16. Close the report.

 **Assessment 3   Creating and Modifying a Form**

Data File

1. With **3-PTCostumeInv.accdb** open, create a form for the CostumeInventory table.
2. Apply a theme of your choosing to the form.
3. Add the logo image **PTLogo-Small.jpg** to the top of the form and then resize the image as needed so that the entire logo is visible.
4. Change the title of the form. You determine appropriate title text and format.
5. Decrease the width of the control objects to improve the appearance and ensure the form will print on standard size paper.
6. Make any other changes you think are necessary to improve the form.
7. Save the form, accepting the default name *CostumeInventory*.
8. Display the first record in the table in Form view and then print the selected record, making sure the form fits on one page.
9. Close the form, saving changes, and then close **3-PTCostumeInv.accdb**.

 **Assessment 4   Finding Information on Creating a Form with a Subform**

Data File

1. Use the Help feature to learn how Access creates a form when the table selected with the Form tool has a one-to-many relationship. ***Hint: Find and read the article titled* Create a form by using the Form tool**.
2. Open **3-WEVendors.accdb** and enable the contents, if necessary.
3. Open the Relationships window and observe that there is a one-to-many relationship between the Vendors (primary) and the Purchases (related) tables.
4. Close the Relationships window.
5. Create a new form using the Form button based on the Vendors table.
6. In Layout view, improve the appearance of the form by applying the skills you have learned in this section.
7. Display the first vendor record in Form view. Print the first record only, making sure the record will require only one page to print.
8. Close the form. Click Yes to save the form and accept the default form name.
9. Close **3-WEVendors.accdb**.

Assessment 5   Researching Movies on the Internet for a New Blog

1. You and your friends are thinking of starting a blog in which you will write reviews for current movies playing in your area. You decide you want to create a database to store records for all of the movies you and your friends will review. Choose four to six movies that are currently playing in your vicinity that you would like to review on your blog. Find the movie websites on the Internet. Look for the information listed in Step 3 that you will be entering into the new database.
2. Create a new database on your storage medium and name it **3-Movies.accdb**.
3. Create a table named *MovieFacts* that will store the following information (you determine the field names and field properties):

Movie Title	Lead Female Actor
Director's Name	Supporting Female Actor
Producer's Name	Movie Category: drama, action, thriller, and so on
Lead Male Actor	Movie Rating: G, PG, R, and so on
Supporting Male Actor	Website Address

4. Create a form to enter the records for the movies you researched. Modify the form by applying the skills you learned in this section.
5. Enter records for the movies you researched using the form created in Step 4.
6. Print only the first record displayed in Form view.
7. Create a report for the MovieFacts table. Modify the report by applying the skills you learned in this section.
8. Print the MovieFacts report.
9. Close **3-Movies.accdb**.

Marquee Challenge

The Waterfront BISTRO

Data Files

Challenge 1   Creating Queries and a Report for a Catering Events Database

1. Dana Hirsch, manager, has provided you with a copy of the database file used to track catering events at the bistro. Dana has been filtering records in the datasheet to obtain the lists needed for managing the events but is finding this process too time consuming. Dana has asked you to figure out how to create queries that can provide the information more efficiently. To begin, open **3-WBSpecialEvents.accdb** and enable the contents, if necessary.
2. Create the following queries:
   a. A WestviewEvents query that displays all events booked in the Westview room. In the query results datasheet, Dana would like the first and last names, the event type, the date the event is booked, the room booked for the event, the number of guests, and the special menu details. Print the query results datasheet using only one page with all column widths adjusted to best fit the entries.
   b. A JuneEvents query that displays all of the events booked in June 2018. In the query results datasheet, show the first and last names, the event type, the date the event is booked, and the room in which the event will be held. (You will need to set the criteria to display events booked between June 1, 2018 and June 30, 2018.) Print the query results datasheet with all column widths adjusted to best fit the entries.

c. An EventRevenue query that displays all records. In the query results datasheet, show the last name, the event type, the date the event is booked, the number of guests, and per-person charge. Calculate in the query the estimated revenue by multiplying the guests by the per person charge. You determine an appropriate column label and format for the calculated column. In the query results datasheet, add a total at the bottom of the calculated column. Print the query results datasheet using only one page and with all column widths adjusted to best fit the entries.

3. Create a report based on the EventRevenue query as shown in Figure WB-3.1 below. The company logo is stored in the file named **TWBLogo-Small.jpg**. Use your best judgment to determine the report formatting elements. The theme used is the default Office theme with individual formatting applied to headings. Apply the Dark Blue background color to the column headings and then apply bold formatting and White font color to the column heading text. Totals can be inserted at the bottom of columns by right-clicking the column heading for which a total is desired and then using options at the shortcut menu. Apply the same formatting to the total in the *Total Revenue* column that you applied to the column headings. Save the report using the default name.

4. Print the report, making sure you use only one page.

5. Close **3-WBSpecialEvents.accdb**.

Figure WB-3.1 Challenge 1

The Waterfront BISTRO	Catering Event Revenue				Monday, November 12, 2018 2:43:35 PM	
Last Name	**Event**	**Date Of Event**	**Guests**	**Per Person Charge**	**Total Revenue**	
Hillmore	Business Meeting	1/15/2018	35	$21.95	$768.25	
Fontaine	Engagement Party	1/20/2018	177	$28.95	$5,124.15	
Corriveau	Birthday Party	1/23/2018	85	$25.95	$2,205.75	
Kressman	Wedding	2/28/2018	266	$28.95	$7,700.70	
Fagan	25th Wedding Anniversary	3/10/2018	88	$28.95	$2,547.60	
Pockovic	Birthday Party	3/18/2018	62	$35.95	$2,228.90	
Gill	Business Meeting	3/29/2018	71	$21.95	$1,558.45	
Bresque	50th Wedding Anniversary	4/12/2018	62	$32.95	$2,042.90	
Santore	Wedding	4/28/2018	157	$25.95	$4,074.15	
Hamid	Engagement Party	5/8/2018	85	$28.95	$2,460.75	
Torrance	Business Meeting	5/15/2018	26	$23.95	$622.70	
Russell	Birthday Party	5/30/2018	36	$26.95	$970.20	
Szucs	Birthday Party	6/10/2018	42	$28.95	$1,215.90	
Griffin	25th Wedding Anniversary	6/17/2018	54	$31.95	$1,725.30	
Doucet	Wedding	6/20/2018	168	$28.95	$4,863.60	
Golinsky	Business Meeting	6/26/2018	57	$24.95	$1,422.15	
Jin Ping	Baby Shower	7/10/2018	62	$21.95	$1,360.90	
McMaster	Engagement Party	7/11/2018	75	$27.95	$2,096.25	
Pavelich	Wedding	7/25/2018	110	$31.95	$3,514.50	
Juanitez	Business Meeting	7/31/2018	49	$23.95	$1,173.55	
			1767		$49,676.65	

Challenge 2   Creating a Form and Report for a Custom Costume Database

1. Bobbie Sinclair, business manager, is pleased with the way the custom costume database is taking shape. Bobbie would now like a form and a report created to facilitate data entry and printing of the custom orders. To begin, open **3-PTCostumes.accdb** and enable the contents, if necessary.
2. Create a form for the CostumeOrders table. You determine the layout and form design by applying skills you learned in this section.
3. With the first record displayed in Form view, print the selected record, making sure you use only one page. Save and close the form, saving changes and accepting the default form name.
4. Create a report to print the CostumeOrders table. You determine the layout and other elements of the report design by applying skills you learned in this section. Consider the example in Figure WB-3.2. In this report, the layout is changed to a stacked arrangement that allows all fields to print on one page since there are numerous fields in the table. To create your report with a similar layout to the one in Figure WB-3.2, explore options on the Report Layout Tools Arrange tab. The report in Figure WB-3.2 is a guide for layout purposes only. Your formatting may vary.
5. Save the report, accepting the default report name, and then print the report, making sure you minimize the amount of paper used.
6. Close **3-PTCostumes.accdb**.

Figure WB-3.2 Challenge 2

Microsoft®

PowerPoint®

Study Tools

Study tools include a presentation and In Brief step lists. Use these resources to help you further develop and review skills learned in this section.

Knowledge Check

 Check your understanding by identifying application tools used in this section. If you are a SNAP user, launch the Knowledge Check from your Assignments page.

Recheck

 Check your understanding by taking this quiz. If you are a SNAP user, launch the Recheck from your Assignments page.

Skills Exercise

 Additional activities are available to SNAP users. If you are a SNAP user, access these activities from your Assignments page.

Skills Review

 Review 1   Creating a Presentation for Marquee Productions

1. With a blank presentation open in PowerPoint, click the Design tab and then click the *Facet* option in the Themes group.
2. Type the title and subtitle for Slide 1 as shown in Figure WB-1.1.
3. Click the Home tab and then click the New Slide button in the Slides group.
4. Type the text shown for Slide 2 in Figure WB-1.1.
5. Continue creating the slides for the presentation as shown in Figure WB-1.1.
6. Insert a new Slide 3 between the current Slides 2 and 3 with the text shown in Figure WB-1.2.
7. Display Slide 2 in the slide pane and then change the slide layout to *Title Slide*.
8. Click in the text *Current Status* to select the placeholder and then move the placeholder up approximately one inch.
9. Click in the text *Overview of project* to select the placeholder and then move the placeholder up approximately one-half inch.
10. Change to Slide Sorter view and then move Slide 3 (*Resources*) immediately after Slide 1 (*Marquee Productions*).
11. Change to Normal view, click the Transitions tab, click the More Transitions button in the gallery in the Transition to This Slide group, and then click the *Orbit* option in the *Dynamic Content* section.

12. Click the *Sound* option box arrow and then click *Drum Roll* at the drop-down list.
13. Click the *Duration* measurement box down arrow until *00.75* displays in the measurement box.
14. Apply the transition, sound, and duration to all slides in the presentation.
15. Save the presentation with the name **1-MPTeamMtg**.
16. Run the slide show beginning with Slide 1.
17. View the presentation as an outline in the Print backstage area.
18. Print the presentation with all five slides displayed horizontally on one page.
19. Save and then close **1-MPTeamMtg.pptx**.

Figure WB-1.1 Review 1

Slide 1	Title	Marquee Productions
	Subtitle	Location Team Meeting
Slide 2	Title	Current Status
	Bullets	• Overview of project
		• Tasks on schedule
		• Tasks behind schedule
Slide 3	Title	Filming Sites
	Bullets	• Gardiner Expressway
		• Kings Mill Park
		• Island Airport
		• Royal Ontario Museum
		• Black Creek Pioneer Village
		• Additional sites
Slide 4	Title	Key Issues
	Bullets	• Equipment rental
		• Budget overruns
		• Transportation concerns
		• Location agreements

Figure WB-1.2 Review 1

Slide 3	Title	Resources
	Bullets	• Location contacts
		• Movie extras
		• Catering company
		• Lodging
		• Transportation rentals

Skills Assessment

 **Assessment 1**   Preparing a Presentation for Worldwide Enterprises

1. Prepare a presentation for Worldwide Enterprises with the information shown in Figure WB-1.3 below. (You determine the design theme.)
2. Add a transition, sound, and transition duration time of your choosing to all slides in the presentation.
3. Run the slide show.
4. Print the presentation with all five slides displayed horizontally on one page.
5. Save the presentation with the name **1-WEExecMtg**.
6. Close **1-WEExecMtg.pptx**.

Figure WB-1.3 Assessment 1

Slide 1	Title	Worldwide Enterprises
	Subtitle	Executive Meeting
Slide 2	Title	Accounting Policies
	Bullets	• Cash equivalents
		• Short-term investments
		• Inventory valuation
		• Property and equipment
		• Foreign currency translation
Slide 3	Title	Financial Instruments
	Bullets	• Investments
		• Derivative instruments
		• Credit risks
		• Fair value of instruments
Slide 4	Title	Inventories
	Bullets	• Products
		• Raw material
		• Equipment
		• Buildings
Slide 5	Title	Employee Plans
	Bullets	• Stock options
		• Bonus plan
		• Savings and retirement plan
		• Defined benefits plan
		• Foreign subsidiaries

Assessment 2 Preparing a Presentation for The Waterfront Bistro

1. Prepare a presentation for The Waterfront Bistro with the information shown in Figure WB-1.4 below. (You determine the design theme.)
2. Add a transition, sound, and transition duration time of your choosing to all slides in the presentation.
3. Run the slide show.
4. Print the presentation with all five slides displayed horizontally on one page.
5. Save the presentation with the name **1-WBServices**.
6. Close **1-WBServices.pptx**.

Figure WB-1.4 Assessment 2

Slide 1	Title	The Waterfront Bistro
	Subtitle	3104 Rivermist Drive
		Buffalo, NY 14280
		(716) 555-3166
Slide 2	Title	Accommodations
	Bullets	• Dining area
		• Salon
		• Two banquet rooms
		• Wine cellar
Slide 3	Title	Menus
	Bullets	• Lunch
		• Dinner
		• Wines
		• Desserts
Slide 4	Title	Catering Services
	Bullets	• Lunch
		– Continental
		– Deli
		– Hot
		• Dinner
		– Vegetarian
		– Meat
		– Seafood
Slide 5	Title	Resource
	Subtitle	Dana Hirsch, Manager

Assessment 3 Finding Information on Setting Slide Show Timings

Data File

1. Open **MPProj.pptx** and then save the presentation with the name **1-MPProj**.
2. Use the Tell Me feature or experiment with the options on the Transitions tab to learn how to set slide show timings manually.
3. Set up the presentation so that, when running the slide show, each slide advances automatically after three seconds.
4. Run the slide show.
5. Save and then close **1-MPProj.pptx**.

Assessment 4   Preparing a Presentation on Cancun, Mexico

1. You are interested in planning a vacation to Cancun, Mexico. Connect to the Internet and search for information on Cancun. Locate information on lodging (hotels), restaurants, activities, and transportation.
2. Using PowerPoint, create a presentation about Cancun that contains the following:
   • Title slide with the title *Vacationing in Cancun* and your name as the subtitle
   • Slide containing the names of at least three major airlines that travel to Cancun
   • Slide containing the names of at least four hotels or resorts in Cancun
   • Slide containing the names of at least four restaurants in Cancun
   • Slide containing at least four activities in Cancun
3. Run the slide show.
4. Print all of the slides on one page.
5. Save the presentation with the name **1-Cancun**.
6. Close **1-Cancun.pptx**.

Marquee Challenge

Challenge 1   Preparing a Presentation on Toronto, Ontario, Canada

1. Create the presentation shown in Figure WB-1.5 on the next page. Apply the Basis design theme and the orange and white color variant. Apply appropriate slide layouts and size and move placeholders so your slides display as shown in the figure. (You will need to increase the size of the subtitle placeholder in Slide 6.)
2. Apply a transition, sound, and transition duration time of your choosing to each slide in the presentation.
3. Save the completed presentation with the name **1-FCTToronto**.
4. Print the presentation as a handout with all six slides displayed horizontally on one page.
5. Close the presentation.

Challenge 2   Preparing a Presentation for Performance Threads

1. Open **PTCostumeMtg.pptx** and then save the presentation with the name **1-PTCostumeMtg**.
2. Apply the Organic design theme, add and rearrange slides, change slide layouts, and move a placeholder so the presentation displays as shown in Figure WB-1.6.
3. Apply a transition, sound, and transition duration time of your choosing to each slide in the presentation.
4. Save and then print the presentation as a handout with all six slides displayed horizontally on one page.
5. Close the presentation.

CITY OF TORONTO

"Diversity is Our Strength"

Museums and Galleries

- Royal Ontario Museum
- Art Gallery of Ontario
- Hockey Hall of Fame and Museum
- Ontario Science Centre
- Bata Shoe Museum

Theatres

- Toronto Centre for the Arts
- Betty Oliphant Theatre
- Massey Hall
- Premiere Dance Theatre
- Roy Thomson Hall
- Royal Alexandra
- Princess of Wales Theatre

continues

Figure WB-1.5 Challenge 1—*continued*

Sports Teams

- Baseball: Toronto Blue Jays
- Hockey: Toronto Maple Leafs
- Basketball: Toronto Raptors
- Football: Toronto Argonauts
- Soccer: Toronto FC

Tours

- Toronto Grand City Tour
- Harbour Cruise
- Toronto Dinner Cruise
- Medieval Times Dinner Show
- Vertical Obsession Helicopter Tour
- Niagara Falls Tour

TORONTO'S NICKNAMES

El Toro

T.O.

T-Dot

Hogtown

Figure WB-1.6 Challenge 2

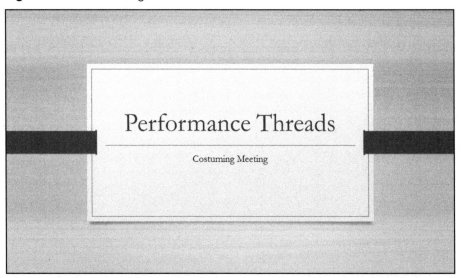

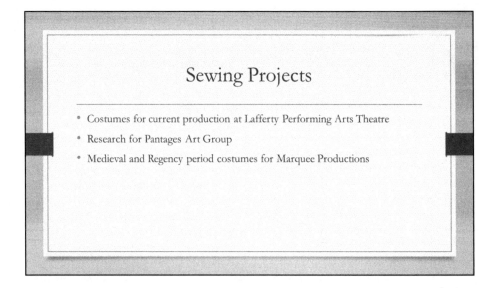

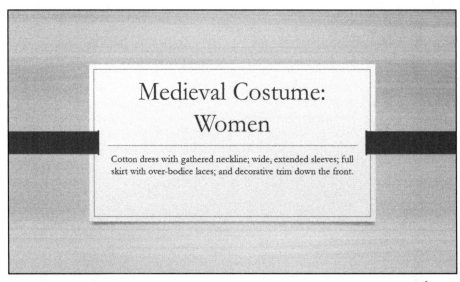

continues

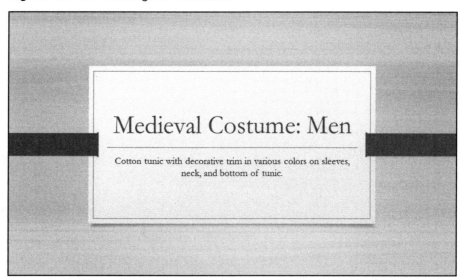

Study Tools

Study tools include a presentation and In Brief step lists. Use these resources to help you further develop and review skills learned in this section.

Knowledge Check

SNAP Check your understanding by identifying application tools used in this section. If you are a SNAP user, launch the Knowledge Check from your Assignments page.

Recheck

SNAP Check your understanding by taking this quiz. If you are a SNAP user, launch the Recheck from your Assignments page.

Skills Exercise

SNAP Additional activities are available to SNAP users. If you are a SNAP user, access these activities from your Assignments page.

Skills Review

Data File

Review 1   Editing and Formatting a Presentation for Marquee Productions

1. Open **MPMeeting.pptx** and then save it with the name **2-MPMeeting**.
2. Apply the Ion Boardroom design theme to the slides in the presentation, change the theme colors to Slipstream, and change the theme fonts to Arial Black - Arial.
3. Delete Slide 5 (contains the title *Financial*) in the slide thumbnails pane.
4. Change to Slide Sorter view and move Slide 7 (*Expenses*) immediately after Slide 3 (*Review of Goals*).
5. Move Slide 6 (*Future Goals*) immediately after the new Slide 7 (*Technology*).
6. Change to Normal view and then make Slide 4 (*Expenses*) the active slide.
7. Decrease the indent of *Payroll* so it displays aligned at the left with *Administration*.
8. Decrease the indent of *Benefits* so it displays aligned at the left with *Payroll* and *Administration*.
9. Make Slide 6 (*Technology*) active and then increase the indent of *Hardware* to the next level, the indent of *Software* to the next level, and the indent of *Technical Support* to the next level.
10. Make Slide 7 (*Future Goals*) active, select the name *Chris Greenbaum*, and then click the Copy button. (Make sure you select only the name and not the space following the name.)
11. Make Slide 3 (*Review of Goals*) active.

12. Move the insertion point immediately to the right of *Overview of Goals*, press the Enter key, press the Tab key, and then click the Paste button. (Clicking the Paste button inserts the name *Chris Greenbaum*. If an extra bullet displays below *Chris Greenbaum*, press the Backspace key two times.)
13. Move the insertion point immediately to the right of *Completed Goals*, press the Enter key, press the Tab key, and then click the Paste button. (Make sure an extra bullet does not display below *Chris Greenbaum*.)
14. Make Slide 7 (*Future Goals*) active, select the name *Shannon Grey* (do not include the space after the name), and then click the Copy button.
15. Make Slide 3 (*Review of Goals*) active and then paste the name *Shannon Grey* below *Goals Remaining* at the same tab location as *Chris Greenbaum*. (Make sure an extra bullet does not display below *Shannon Grey*.)
16. Paste the name *Shannon Grey* below *Analysis/Discussion* at the same tab location as *Chris Greenbaum*. (Make sure an extra bullet does not display below *Shannon Grey*.)
17. Make Slide 1 active, select the text *Marquee Productions*, change the font to Candara, change the font size to 60 points, and then apply bold formatting.
18. Select the text *ANNUAL MEETING*, change the font to Candara, change the font size to 36 points, and then apply bold formatting.
19. Make Slide 2 (*Agenda*) active, select the title *Agenda*, change the font to Candara, change the font size to 48 points, and then apply bold formatting.
20. Using Format Painter, apply the same formatting to the title in each of the remaining slides.
21. Make Slide 6 (*Technology*) active, select all of the bulleted text, and then change the line spacing to 1.5 lines.
22. Make Slide 8 (*Proposals*) active, select all of the bulleted text, and then change the spacing before paragraphs to 24 points.
23. Make Slide 2 (*Agenda*) active and then insert the image shown in Figure WB-2.1 with the following specifications:
    • Use the Pictures button on the Insert tab to insert the **Bullseye.png** image.
    • Apply the Blue, Accent color 1 Light color to the image (second column, third row in the *Recolor* section).
    • Change the height of the image to 4 inches.
    • Position the image as shown in the figure.
24. Make Slide 4 (*Expenses*) active and then insert the **DollarSymbol.png** image. Apply the Blue, Accent color 1 Light color to the image and change the height of the image to 3.3 inches. Position the image as shown in Figure WB-2.2.
25. Apply a transition, sound, and transition duration time to all slides in the presentation.
26. Run the slide show.
27. Print the presentation as handouts with four slides displayed horizontally per page.
28. Save and then close **2-MPMeeting.pptx**.

Figure WB-2.1 Review 1, Slide 2

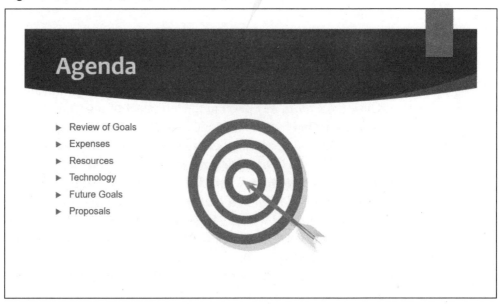

Figure WB-2.2 Review 1, Slide 4

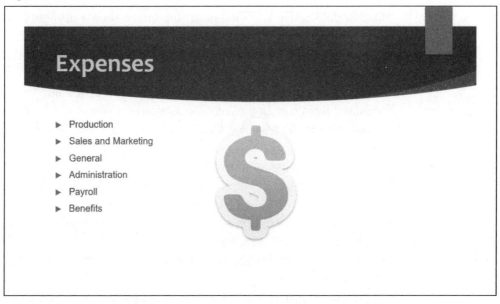

Review 2   Formatting a Presentation for Performance Threads

1. Open **PTPres.pptx** and then save it with the name **2-PTPres**.
2. Change the slide size to Standard (4:3) and ensure the fit.
3. Change the design theme to Organic and the theme colors to Red.
4. With Slide 1 active, insert the **PTLogo.jpg** file. (Use the Pictures button in the Images group on the Insert tab.) Change the height of the logo to 2 inches and then position the logo in the middle of the slide.
5. Make the background of the logo transparent by clicking the Color button on the Picture Tools Format tab, clicking the *Set Transparent Color* option at the dropdown gallery, and then clicking anywhere in the white background of the logo.

6. Make Slide 3 active, select the bulleted text, and then change the line spacing to 1.5 lines.

7. Make Slide 4 active, select the bulleted text, and then change the spacing after paragraphs to 18 points.

8. Make Slide 2 active and then insert the SmartArt organizational chart shown in Figure WB-2.3 on the next page with the following specifications:
   - Click the *Hierarchy* option in the left panel of the Choose a SmartArt Graphic dialog box and then double-click the *Organization Chart* option.
   - Delete and add boxes so your organization chart has the same boxes as the one in Figure WB-2.3. ***Hint: Delete the single box in the middle row, delete one of the boxes in the bottom row, and then use the Add Shape button arrow and click Add Shape Below to add the boxes in the bottom row.***
   - Type the text in the boxes. (Press Shift + Enter after entering the names.)
   - Apply the Colorful - Accent Colors color to the organizational chart (first option in the *Colorful* section).
   - Apply the Cartoon SmartArt style to the organizational chart (third column, first row in the *3-D* section).
   - Apply the Fill - Black, Text 1, Shadow WordArt style to the text in the shapes (first column, first row).

9. Make Slide 3 active and then insert the image shown in Figure WB-2.4 on the next page with the following specifications:
   - Use the Pictures button on the Insert tab to insert the **Medical.png** image.
   - Change the height of the image to 2.9 inches.
   - Change the color of the image to Dark Red, Accent color 1 Light (second column, third row in the *Recolor* section).
   - Apply the Brightness: 0% (Normal) Contrast: +40% brightness and contrast (third column, fifth row).
   - Position the image as shown in Figure WB-2.4.

10. Make Slide 5 active and then insert the SmartArt graphic shown in Figure WB-2.5 on the next page with the following specifications:
    - Click the *Process* option in the left panel at the Choose a SmartArt Graphic dialog box and then double-click *Alternating Flow*.
    - Apply the Colorful - Accent Colors color to the graphic (first option in the *Colorful* section).
    - Apply the Cartoon SmartArt style to the graphic (third column, first row in the *3-D* section).
    - Type the text in the boxes as shown in Figure WB-2.5.

11. Make Slide 2 active, click the SmartArt organizational chart, and then animate the organizational chart using options on the Animations tab. (You determine the type of animation.)

12. Make Slide 5 active, click the SmartArt graphic, and then animate the graphic using options on the Animations tab. (You determine the type of animation.)

13. Make Slide 3 active, click the bulleted text, and then apply the Split animation.

14. Make Slide 4 active, click the bulleted text, and then apply the Split animation.

15. Run the slide show.

16. Print the presentation as handouts with all five slides displayed horizontally on one page.

17. Save and then close **2-PTPres.pptx**.

Figure WB-2.3 Review 2, Slide 2

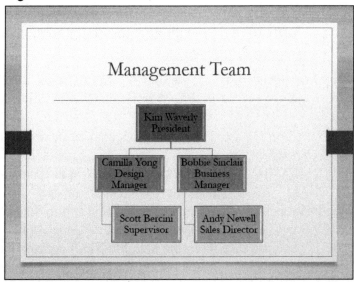

Figure WB-2.4 Review 2, Slide 3

Figure WB-2.5 Review 2, Slide 5

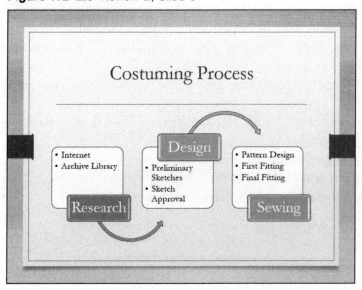

Skills Assessment

NIAGARA
PENINSULA
COLLEGE

Data Files

Assessment 1 Formatting a Presentation for Niagara Peninsula College,
Theatre Arts Division

1. Open **NPCTheatreArts.pptx** and then save it with the name **2-NPCTheatreArts**.
2. Move Slide 7 (*ASSOCIATE DEGREES*) immediately after Slide 2 (*MISSION STATEMENT*).
3. Move Slide 6 (*SEMESTER COSTS*) immediately after the new Slide 7 (*FALL SEMESTER CLASSES*).
4. Make Slide 2 (*MISSION STATEMENT*) active, click in the paragraph below the title *MISSION STATEMENT*, and then justify the text alignment.
5. Change the line spacing to 1.5 lines for the bulleted text in Slides 5 and 7.
6. Make Slide 5 active, select the bulleted text, and then apply italic formatting.
7. Make Slide 1 active and then insert the logo file **NPCLogo.jpg** into the slide. Increase the size of the logo, set the background color as transparent, and then position the logo at the left side of the slide in the gray portion. *Hint: Use the Color button in the Adjust group on the Picture Tools Format tab to set the background color as transparent.*
8. Make Slide 3 active and then insert a Radial Cycle SmartArt graphic (located in the *Cycle* category in the Choose a SmartArt Graphic dialog box) in the slide. Insert the text *Theatre Arts Division* in the middle circle and then insert the following text in the remaining four circles: *Production, Acting, Set Design,* and *Interactive Media*. Apply a color and SmartArt style of your choosing to the graphic. Apply any other formatting to enhance the appearance of the graphic. Position the graphic attractively on the slide.
9. Make Slide 4 active and then insert the Organization Chart SmartArt graphic (located in the *Hierarchy* category in the Choose a SmartArt Graphic dialog box) in the slide with the boxes and text shown in Figure WB-2.6. *Hint: To add the extra box along the bottom, click the left box at the bottom, click the Add Shape button arrow, and then click* **Add Shape Before.** Apply a color and SmartArt style of your choosing to the organizational chart. Apply any other formatting you desire to enhance the appearance of the organizational chart. Position the chart attractively on the slide.
10. Make Slide 7 active and then insert the **Money.png** image in the slide. Size, position, and recolor the image so it enhances the slide.
11. Make Slide 3 active and then apply an animation of your choosing to the SmartArt graphic.
12. Make Slide 4 active and then apply an animation of your choosing to the organizational chart.
13. Apply a transition, sound, and transition duration time of your choosing to all slides in the presentation.
14. Run the slide show.
15. Print the presentation as handouts with four slides displayed horizontally per page.
16. Save and then close **2-NPCTheatreArts.pptx**.

Figure WB-2.6 Assessment 1, SmartArt Organizational Chart

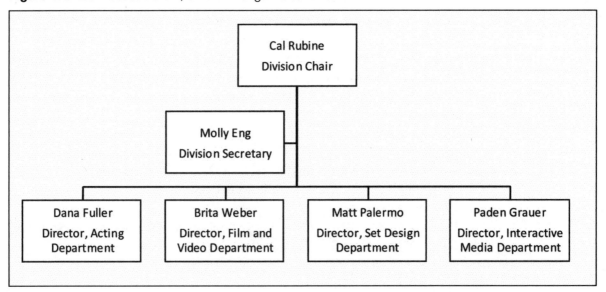

Assessment 2 Formatting a Presentation for First Choice Travel

1. Open **FCTVacations.pptx** and then save it with the name **2-FCTVacations**.
2. Display the Format Background task pane and make sure the fill options display. Apply the Radial Gradient - Accent 1 gradient fill color (first column, fifth row) and then apply the gradient fill to all slides in the presentation. *Hint: Use the Preset gradients button with the* **Gradient fill** *option selected in the Format Background task pane.*
3. Increase the font size of the subtitle *Vacation Specials* in Slide 1. (You determine the size.)
4. Apply bold formatting, the Gold, Accent 5, Lighter 80% font color (ninth column, second row in *Theme Colors* section), and left alignment to each heading in Slides 2 through 6.
5. Make Slide 1 active and then insert the **FCTLogo.jpg** file into the slide. Make the background of the logo transparent. You determine the size and position of the logo.
6. Apply any formatting you feel is necessary to improve the appearance of each slide.
7. Apply a transition and sound to each slide in the presentation.
8. Run the slide show.
9. Print the presentation as handouts with all six slides displayed horizontally on one page.
10. Save **2-FCTVacations.pptx**.

Assessment 3 Using the Tell Me Feature to Convert Text to a SmartArt Graphic

1. With **2-FCTVacations.pptx** open, make Slide 4 active and select all of the bulleted text.
2. Use the Tell Me feature to convert the bulleted text to a SmartArt graphic of your choosing.
3. Apply formatting to enhance the appearance of the SmartArt graphic.
4. Print only Slide 4.
5. Save and then close **2-FCTVacations.pptx**.

Assessment 4   Locating Information and Preparing a Presentation

1. Search for information on the Internet on your favorite author, historical figure, or entertainer.
2. Using PowerPoint, create a presentation with a minimum of four slides on the person you chose. Include a title slide with the person's name and your name and additional slides with information such as personal statistics, achievements, and awards.
3. Take an appropriate screenshot image of the person or something related to the person and insert it into any slide where it seems appropriate.
4. Apply a transition and sound to each slide in the presentation.
5. Save the presentation and name it **2-PerPres**.
6. Run the slide show.
7. Print the slides as handouts with six slides displayed horizontally per page.
8. Save and then close **2-PerPres.pptx**.

Marquee Challenge

Challenge 1   Preparing a Presentation for Worldwide Enterprises

1. Create the presentation shown in Figure WB-2.7. Apply the Retrospect design theme and the Blue II theme colors. Insert **WELogo.jpg** in Slide 1. In Slide 2, apply the Blue, Accent 2 font color (sixth column, first row in the *Theme Colors* section) to the title text and the Dark Blue font color (ninth option in the *Standard Colors* section) to the subtitle text. Insert the **Stockmarket.png** image in Slide 3. Change the color of the image to Blue, Accent color 2 Light (third column, third row in the *Recolor* section). Size and position the image as shown in the figure. Insert the **Package.png** image in Slide 6. Change the brightness and contrast to Brightness: +20% Contrast: -20% (fourth column, second row in the *Brightness/Contrast* section). Size and position the images as shown in the figure. Create and format the SmartArt graphic shown in Slide 5.
2. Save the completed presentation and name it **2-WEDist**.
3. Print the presentation as a handout with all six slides displayed horizontally on one page and then close the presentation.

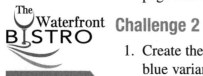

Challenge 2   Preparing a Presentation for The Waterfront Bistro

1. Create the presentation shown in Figure WB-2.8. Apply the Dividend theme and the blue variant (second option in the Variants group). Change the slide size to Standard (4:3) and ensure fit. Insert **TWBLogo.jpg** in Slides 1 and 2 and then apply the Drop Shadow Rectangle picture style to the logo on both slides. Create and format the SmartArt organizational chart in Slide 3 using the Hierarchy SmartArt graphic. Create and format the SmartArt graphic shown in Slide 4. Insert the **Catering.png** image in Slide 6 and format and size the image as shown in the figure.
2. Save the completed presentation and name it **2-TWBInfo**.
3. Print the presentation as a handout with all six slides displayed horizontally on one page and then close the presentation.

Distribution Department

PLANNING MEETING

Market

Market share

Current market

Future market

Market indicators

Consumer profile

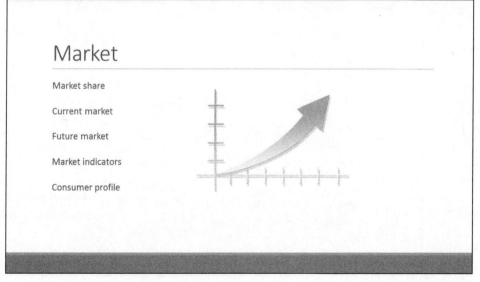

continues

Figure WB-2.7 Challenge 1—*continued*

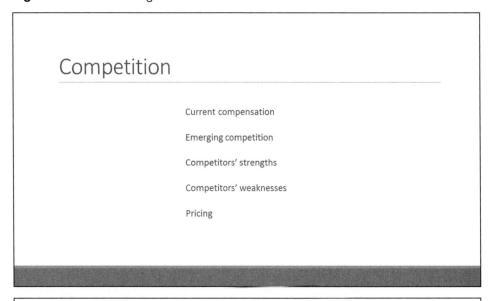

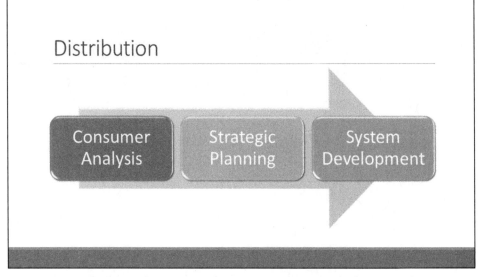

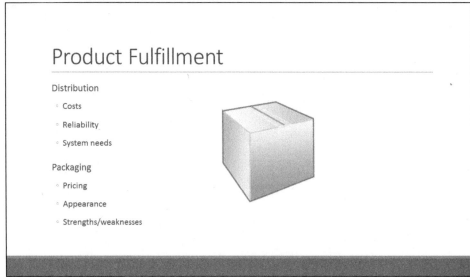

Figure WB-2.8 Challenge 2

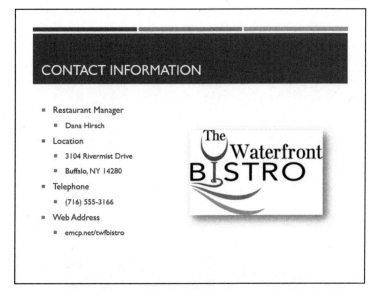

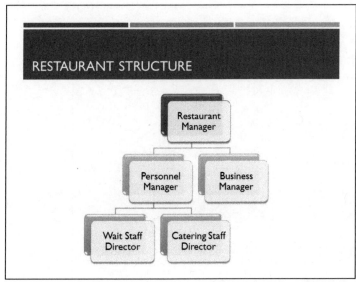

continues

Figure WB-2.8 Challenge 2—*continued*

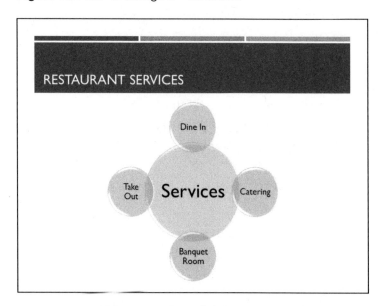

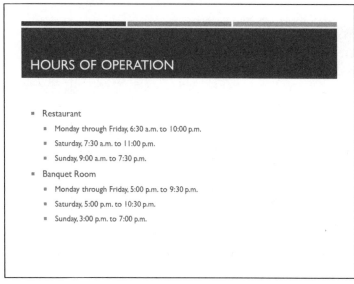

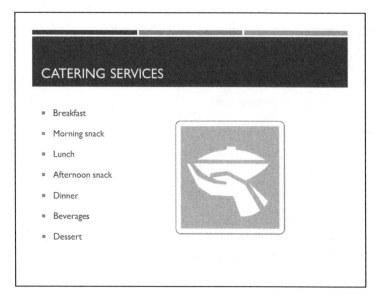

Study Tools

Study tools include a PowerPoint presentation and In Brief step lists. Use these resources to help you further develop and review skills learned in this section.

Recheck

Check your understanding by taking this quiz. If you are a SNAP user, launch the Recheck from your Assignments page.

Skills Review

Review 1   Exporting Access Data to Excel

1. Open **IB-PTCostumes.accdb** and then enable the contents.
2. Click *CostumeInventory* in the Tables group in the Navigation pane and then export the data to Excel with formatting and layout. Specify you want the file to open after exporting. Save the workbook with the name **IB-CostumeInventory**.
3. When the data displays in Excel, make the following changes in the specified cells:
   - C4:   Change *110.00* to *120.00*.
   - C5:   Change *110.00* to *125.00*.
   - C7:   Change *99.50* to *105.00*.
4. Save, print, and then close **IB-CostumeInventory.xlsx**.
5. Click the Access button on the taskbar.
6. Close the Export - Excel Spreadsheet dialog box.

Review 2   Exporting an Access Report to Word

1. Make sure Access is active and **IB-PTCostumes.accdb** is open.
2. Click *CostumeInventory* in the Reports group in the Navigation pane and then export it to a Word document specifying you want the file to open after exporting. Save the document as **IB-CostumeInventory**.
3. When the data displays in Word, change the page layout to landscape orientation, and change the margins to *Normal*.
4. Save, print, and close **IB-CostumeInventory.rtf**.
5. Make Access active and then close the Export - RTF File dialog box.

Review 3   Importing Data to a New Table

1. In Access, make sure **IB-PTCostumes.accdb** is open.
2. Import a worksheet from the Excel workbook named **PTCostumeHours.xlsx**. At the first Import Spreadsheet Wizard dialog box, make sure the *First Row Contains Column Headings* option contains a check mark. Do not make any changes to the second dialog box. Click the *No primary key* option at the third dialog box. At the

fourth dialog box, type DesignHours in the *Import to Table* text box and then click the Finish button. At the message asking if you want to save the import steps, click the Close button.
3. Open the new DesignHours table.
4. Print and then close the DesignHours table.
5. Close the **IB-PTCostumes.accdb** database.

Data File

Review 4 Exporting a PowerPoint Presentation to Word

1. Make sure Word and PowerPoint are open.
2. Make PowerPoint active, open **FCTVacations.pptx**, and then save it with the name **IB-FCTVacations**.
3. Send the PowerPoint data to Word as slides with blank lines next to the slides. Click the *Blank lines next to slides* option and the *Paste link* option at the Send to Microsoft Word dialog box.
4. Save the Word document with the name **IB-FCTVacSpecials**.
5. Print and then close **IB-FCTVacSpecials.docx**.
6. Click the PowerPoint button on the taskbar.
7. Make Slide 4 active and then change *$1,150* to *$1,250*, change *$1,275* to *$1,375*, and change *$1,315* to *$1,415*.
8. Save the presentation and then print Slide 4.
9. Make Word active, open **IB-FCTVacSpecials.docx**, and then click Yes at the question asking if you want to update the link.
10. Print only page 2 of **IB-FCTVacSpecials.docx**.
11. Save and then close the document.
12. Make PowerPoint active and then close **IB-FCTVacations.pptx**.

NIAGARA
PENINSULA
COLLEGE

Data Files

Review 5 Linking and Editing an Excel Chart in a PowerPoint Slide

1. With PowerPoint active, open **NPCEnroll.pptx** and then save it with the name **IB-NPCEnroll**.
2. Make Slide 4 active.
3. Make Excel active, open **NPCEnrollChart.xlsx**, and then save it with the name **IB-NPCEnrollChart**.
4. Click the chart once to select it (make sure you select the entire chart and not a chart element) and then copy and link the chart to Slide 4 in the **IB-NPCEnroll.pptx** PowerPoint presentation. (Be sure to use the Paste Special dialog box to link the chart.)
5. Increase the size of the chart to better fill the slide and then center the chart on the slide.
6. Click outside the chart to deselect it.
7. Save the presentation, print Slide 4, and then close the presentation.
8. Click the Excel button on the taskbar.
9. Click outside the chart to deselect it.
10. Save and then print **IB-NPCEnrollChart.xlsx**.
11. Insert another department in the worksheet (and chart) by making cell A7 active, clicking the Insert button arrow in the Cells group on the Home tab, and then clicking *Insert Sheet Rows* at the drop-down list. (This creates a new row 7.) Type the following text in the specified cells:

A7:	Directing	C7:	32
B7:	18	D7:	25

12. Click in cell A4.
13. Save, print, and then close **IB-NPCEnrollChart.xlsx**.
14. Make PowerPoint active and then open **IB-NPCEnroll.pptx**. At the message telling you that the presentation contains links, click the Update Links button.
15. Display Slide 4 and then notice the change to the chart.
16. Save the presentation, print only Slide 4, and then close the presentation.

Review 6 Embedding and Editing a Word Table in a PowerPoint Slide

1. With PowerPoint active, open **IB-NPCEnroll.pptx**. At the message telling you that the presentation contains links, click the Update Links button.
2. Make Slide 5 the active slide.
3. Make Word active and then open **NPCContacts.docx**.
4. Select the table and then copy and embed it in Slide 5 in the **IB-NPCEnroll.pptx** presentation. (Make sure you use the Paste Special dialog box.)
5. With the table selected in the slide, use the sizing handles to increase the size and change the position of the table so it better fills the slide.
6. Click outside the table to deselect it and then save the presentation.
7. Double-click the table, select *Editing* in the name *Emerson Editing*, and type Edits.
8. Click outside the table to deselect it.
9. Print Slide 5 of the presentation.
10. Apply a transition and transition sound of your choosing to all slides in the presentation.
11. Run the slide show.
12. Save and close **IB-NPCEnroll.pptx** and then close PowerPoint.
13. Close the Word document **NPCContacts.docx**.

Review 7 Linking Data to a New Table and Editing Linked Data

1. Make Excel active, open **FCTBookings.xlsx**, and then save it with the name **IB-FCTBookings.xlsx**.
2. Open **IB-FCTCommissions.accdb** and then enable the contents.
3. Link the Excel workbook **IB-FCTBookings.xlsx** with the **IB-FCTCommissions.accdb** database. (At the Get External Data - Excel Spreadsheet dialog box, click the *Link to the data source by creating a linked table* option. At the second Link Spreadsheet Wizard dialog box, type LinkedCommissions in the *Linked Table Name* text box.)
4. Open, print, and then close the new LinkedCommissions table.
5. Click the Excel button on the taskbar.
6. Make cell C2 active, type the formula =b2*0.03, and then press the Enter key.
7. Make cell C2 active and then use the fill handle to copy the formula down to cell C13.
8. Save, print, and then close **IB-FCTBookings.xlsx**.
9. Click the Access button on the taskbar.
10. Open the LinkedCommissions table.
11. Save, print, and then close the LinkedCommissions table.
12. Close **IB-FCTCommissions.accdb** and then close Access.

Review 8   Embedding an Object

1. Make Word active, open **WERevMemo.docx**, and then save it with the name **IB-WERevMemo**.
2. Make Excel active and then open **WEExcelRev.xlsx**.
3. Embed the data in cells A2 through D8 in the Word document a double space below the paragraph of text in the body of the memo.
4. Save and then print **IB-WERevMemo.docx**.
5. Click the Excel button on the taskbar, close the workbook, and then close Excel.
6. With **IB-WERevMemo.docx** open, double-click the worksheet and then make the following changes to the data in the specified cells:

    A2:   Change *July Revenues* to *August Revenues*.
    B4:   Change *1,356,000* to *1,575,000*.
    B5:   Change *2,450,000* to *2,375,000*.
    B6:   Change *1,635,000* to *1,750,000*.
    B7:   Change *950,000* to *1,100,000*.
    B8:   Change *1,050,000* to *1,255,000*.

7. Click in cell A2 and then click outside the worksheet to deselect it.
8. Make the following changes to the memo: change the date from *August 14, 2018* to *September 2, 2018*, and change the subject from *July Revenues* to *August Revenues*.
9. Save, print, and then close **IB-WERevMemo.docx**.
10. Close Word.